SRa Art Connections

Art Across the Curriculum

Level 5

SRA McGraw-Hill

Columbus, Ohio

A Division of The McGraw·Hill Companies

Cover: Katsushika Hokusai. (Japanese). *The Great Wave off Kanagawa. 36 Views of Mount Fuji.* 1831–1833. Polychrome woodblock print. 10 $\frac{1}{8}$ × 14 $\frac{15}{16}$ inches. Metropolitan Museum of Art, New York, New York. **Back Cover,** top, **Dustin Sandidge,** Age 11, *Night City,* middle, **Tiffany Hayes,** Age 9, *The Encounter,* bottom, **Robert Landers,** Age 11, *Rainbow over the Mountains*

SRA/McGraw-Hill

A Division of The **McGraw·Hill** *Companies*

Printed in the United States of America.

Send all inquiries to:
SRA/McGraw-Hill
250 Old Wilson Bridge Road
Suite 310
Worthington, Ohio 43085

ISBN 0-02-688337-6
   3 4 5 6 7 8 9 PAT 01 00 99 98

Table of Contents

Introduction to Art Across the Curriculum..ix
   The Reading/Language Arts Connections...x
   The Mathematics Connections...xi
   The Science Connections..xii
   The Social Studies Connections...xiii
   The Arts Connections..xiv
   The Technology Connections...xv

Unit 1 Blackline Masters
   Unit 1, Lesson 1: Lines
      Reading/Language Arts: Understanding Words by Their Histories...........................1
      Mathematics: Division Patterns...2
      Science: Planning to Recycle...3
      Social Studies: Contrasting Industrial and Earlier Cultures..............................4
      Arts (Dance): Lines in a Dance..5
      Technology: Lines..6
   Unit 1, Lesson 2: Geometric and Free-Form Shapes
      Reading/Language Arts: Free Verse Poetry..7
      Mathematics: Using Geometric Shapes...8
      Science: Understanding Migration..9
      Social Studies: Using Shapes to Graph Facts..10
      Arts (Music): Writing a Song..11
      Technology: Geometric and Free-Form Shapes...12
   Unit 1, Lesson 3: Value in Shading
      Reading/Language Arts: Explaining a Paradox...13
      Mathematics: Ratios..14
      Science: Understanding Needs for Survival...15
      Social Studies: Purposes of Political Parties...16
      Arts (Theater): Creating Illusion Onstage...17
      Technology: Value in Shading..18
   Unit 1, Lesson 4: Value in Lines
      Reading/Language Arts: Writing to Express Emotion......................................19
      Mathematics: Using Ordered Pairs to Locate Regions...................................20
      Science: Investigating Value...21
      Social Studies: Sharecropping and the Southern Economy.............................22
      Arts (Music): Understanding Spirituals...23
      Technology: Value in Lines...24

Unit 1, Lesson 5: Value

Reading/Language Arts: A Unified Composition..25

Mathematics: Finding Volume..26

Science: Reflected Light and Mirrors..27

Social Studies: Using Maps to Learn History..28

Arts (Music): Music Culture Then and Now..29

Technology: Value..30

Unit 1, Lesson 6: Value Contrast

Reading/Language Arts: Creating Interest and Variety in Sentences...............31

Mathematics: Measuring to Create a Pattern..32

Science: Mass, Force, and Movement..33

Social Studies: Technology and the Automobile..34

Arts (Theater): The Stage..35

Technology: Value..36

Unit 2 Blackline Masters

Unit 2, Lesson 1: Monochromatic Colors

Reading/Language Arts: Biography..37

Mathematics: Calculating Distances on a Map..38

Science: Solving a Map-Making Problem..39

Social Studies: Researching Martin Luther King, Jr. 40

Arts (Music): Songs That Celebrate Your State..41

Technology: Monochromatic Colors..42

Unit 2, Lesson 2: Analogous Colors

Reading/Language Arts: Describing a Painting..43

Mathematics: Adding Decimals..44

Science: Making a Loom and Weaving..45

Social Studies: Reading a Topographic Map..46

Arts (Music): Rhythm and Repetition..47

Technology: Analogous Colors..48

Unit 2, Lesson 3: Complementary Colors

Reading/Language Arts: Supporting Opinions with Facts..49

Mathematics: Building Geometric Shapes..50

Science: Understanding the Past from Data..51

Social Studies: Textiles in Different Eras..52

Arts (Dance): How Costume Adds to a Dance..53

Technology: Complementary Colors..54

Unit 2, Lesson 4: Warm and Cool Colors

Reading/Language Arts: Using the Dictionary..55

Mathematics: Estimating..56

Science: Stargazing..57

Social Studies: Murals and Mexico..58

Arts (Theater): Using Research to Develop a Script..59

Technology: Warm and Cool Colors..60

Unit 2, Lesson 5: Visual Rhythm and Movement

Reading/Language Arts: Hieroglyphics..61

Mathematics: Calendars for Measuring Time..62

Science: Changes from Combining Materials..63

Social Studies: Adapting to Life in a Hot, Dry Land..64

Arts (Dance): Contrasting Dance Movements..65

Technology: Visual Rhythm and Movement..66

Unit 2, Lesson 6: Color and Visual Rhythm

Reading/Language Arts: Preparing to Research.................................67

Mathematics: Estimating...68

Science: Designing Shoes...69

Social Studies: Lives of Pioneers...70

Arts (Theater): Writing Dialogue for Contrasting Characters..............71

Technology: Visual Rhythm and Movement......................................72

Unit 3 Blackline Masters

Unit 3, Lesson 1: Positive and Negative Space

Reading/Language Arts: Reading to Learn.......................................73

Mathematics: Measuring Space..74

Science: Patterns in Nature...75

Social Studies: Pablo Picasso's Homeland.......................................76

Arts (Theater): Dramatic Reversals..77

Technology: Positive and Negative Space...78

Unit 3, Lesson 2: Positive and Negative Space Reversal

Reading/Language Arts: Creating Illusion in Writing..........................79

Mathematics: Looking for Patterns...80

Science: Reptiles in Danger...81

Social Studies: A Country Claimed from the Sea..............................82

Arts (Dance): Animal Moves..83

Technology: Positive and Negative Space Reversal.............................84

Unit 3, Lesson 3: Texture

Reading/Language Arts: Expressing Thoughts Through Writing............85

Mathematics: Decorative Math...86

Science: A Cleaner Source of Energy...87

Social Studies: Texture in Textiles..88

Arts (Music): Texture in a Ballad..89

Technology: Texture..90

Unit 3, Lesson 4: Architectural Form and Texture

Reading/Language Arts: Form Shapes Communication........................91

Mathematics: Faraway Planets...92

Science: Exercise for Health...93

Social Studies: Topographical Maps..94

Arts (Music): Music of Space...95

Technology: Architectural Form and Texture....................................96

Unit 3, Lesson 5: Architectural Shape and Visual Texture

Reading/Language Arts: Building Understanding................................97

Mathematics: Using Math to Build..98

Science: Investigate to Solve a Problem...99

Social Studies: Homes That Fit...100

Arts (Dance): Moving Together to Build a Dance.............................101

Technology: Architectural Shape and Visual Texture.........................102

Unit 3, Lesson 6: Form and Tactile Texture

Reading/Language Arts: Make Yourself Clear...................................103

Mathematics: Data That Describe Australia.....................................104

Science: Changes Occur Over Time..105

Social Studies: Using Everyday Knowledge to Solve Problems............106

Arts (Theater): What Does It Feel Like?..107
Technology: Form and Tactile Texture..108

Unit 4 Blackline Masters
   Unit 4, Lesson 1: Proportion
      Reading/Language Arts: Keeping Things in Proportion.....................109
      Mathematics: In Proportion..110
      Science: Seeing in Color..111
      Social Studies: First Steps Toward Democracy.....................112
      Arts (Theater): Expressing Thoughts in a Monologue...............113
      Technology: Proportion..114
   Unit 4, Lesson 2: Scale
      Reading/Language Arts: Write a Conversation.....................115
      Mathematics: Geometric Forms in Architecture....................116
      Science: The Himalayan Ecosystem..................................117
      Social Studies: Graphing Mountain Heights........................118
      Arts (Theater): Using Scale to Make a Point.....................119
      Technology: Scale..120
   Unit 4, Lesson 3: Facial Proportions
      Reading/Language Arts: Write a Letter to an Artist..............121
      Mathematics: Symmetry...122
      Science: Get a Sense of Your World................................123
      Social Studies: Pioneers in the Women's Movement................124
      Arts (Music): Matching Mood to Music.............................125
      Technology: Facial Proportions...................................126
   Unit 4, Lesson 4: Exaggeration
      Reading/Language Arts: Synonyms in Descriptions.................127
      Mathematics: Comparing Prices....................................128
      Science: Rocks and Minerals as Art Materials....................129
      Social Studies: Map of Colombia..................................130
      Arts (Dance): Exaggerated Movements.............................131
      Technology: Exaggeration..132
   Unit 4, Lesson 5: Distortion
      Reading/Language Arts: Listening for Distortion.................133
      Mathematics: Topology..134
      Science: Animals and Their Environments..........................135
      Social Studies: How One Culture Has Adapted to Change...........136
      Arts (Music): Effects of Distorted Sound.......................137
      Technology: Distortion..138
   Unit 4, Lesson 6: Scale and Proportion
      Reading/Language Arts: Create a Lifelike Character..............139
      Mathematics: Ratio...140
      Science: Home and School Safety..................................141
      Social Studies: Vasco Núñez de Balboa, Conquistador............142
      Arts (Theater): Encounter with a Sculpture.....................143
      Technology: Scale and Proportion................................144

Unit 5 Blackline Masters
   Unit 5, Lesson 1: Formal Balance
      Reading/Language Arts: Balance in Sentences....................145

Mathematics: Flips, Slides, and Rotations...146
Science: Flower Reproduction..147
Social Studies: Robots and Society...148
Arts (Dance): Robot Dance...149
Technology: Formal Balance...150

Unit 5, Lesson 2: Informal Balance
Reading/Language Arts: Changes in Language......................................151
Mathematics: Finding an Unknown to Balance an Equation..........................152
Science: Force and Motion..153
Social Studies: Machines and Society...154
Arts (Theater): Circus Characters..155
Technology: Informal Balance..156

Unit 5, Lesson 3: Radial Balance
Reading/Language Arts: Editing a Draft..157
Mathematics: Completing Patterns..158
Science: Recording Data Accurately..159
Social Studies: Colonial Folk Art—Useful Things.................................160
Arts (Music): Folk Songs...161
Technology: Radial Balance..162

Unit 5, Lesson 4: Perspective Techniques
Reading/Language Arts: Describing From Up Close, From Far Away...................163
Mathematics: Reading a Schedule...164
Science: Steam Power...165
Social Studies: Transporting People...166
Arts (Theater): Developing a Character..167
Technology: Perspective Techniques..168

Unit 5, Lesson 5: Linear Perspective
Reading/Language Arts: Farm Journal...169
Mathematics: Garden Fractions...170
Science: A Changing Landscape...171
Social Studies: Architectural and Cultural Values..............................172
Arts (Music): Songs Reflect Societies...173
Technology: Linear Perspective..174

Unit 5, Lesson 6: Point of View and Direct Observation
Reading/Language Arts: Point of View in a Story.................................175
Mathematics: Identifying Forms from Different Angles.............................176
Science: Safe Levels of Sound...177
Social Studies: Railroads and U.S. Expansion....................................178
Arts (Music): Railroad Songs..179
Technology: Point of View and Direct Observation................................180

Unit 6 Blackline Masters
Unit 6, Lesson 1: Emphasis Through Contrast
Reading/Language Arts: Contrasts in Language....................................181
Mathematics: Grid Location and Emphasis in a Design.............................182
Science: Identifying Clouds and Predicting Weather..............................183
Social Studies: The Rodeo and Western Culture...................................184
Arts (Dance): Creating Contrast in Dance..185
Technology: Emphasis Through Contrast...186

Unit 6, Lesson 2: Emphasis as a Focal Point

Reading/Language Arts: The Focus of a Paragraph.......................187

Mathematics: Measurements and Calculations to String a Loom.....................188

Science: Characteristics of Wool.......................189

Social Studies: Changes in the Navajo Culture.......................190

Arts (Music): Emphasis in Music.......................191

Technology: Emphasis as a Focal Point.......................192

Unit 6, Lesson 3: Variety

Reading/Language Arts: Inventing a Story from Details.......................193

Mathematics: Possible Combinations.......................194

Science: A Recycling Project.......................195

Social Studies: Information Gathering.......................196

Arts (Theater): Character and Conflict.......................197

Technology: Variety.......................198

Unit 6, Lesson 4: Harmony

Reading/Language Arts: Elements That Unify a Poem.......................199

Mathematics: Similar and Congruent Figures.......................200

Science: Interactions within an Ecosystem.......................201

Social Studies: Living in Balance with Nature.......................202

Arts (Music): Chords and Harmony.......................203

Technology: Harmony.......................204

Unit 6, Lesson 5: Environmental Unity

Reading/Language Arts: Subject–Verb Agreement.......................205

Mathematics: Estimating Distances.......................206

Science: Levers and Force.......................207

Social Studies: Rights and Responsibilities.......................208

Arts (Theater): Pantomiming Harmony and Conflict.......................209

Technology: Environmental Unity.......................210

Unit 6, Lesson 6: Unity

Reading/Language Arts: Unified Paragraphs.......................211

Mathematics: Measuring to Make a Pattern.......................212

Science: The Mineral Quartz.......................213

Social Studies: Our Love of Necklaces.......................214

Arts (Theater): The Mystery of the Missing Necklace.......................215

Technology: Unity.......................216

Answer Key.......................217

Introduction

What Is *Art Across the Curriculum?*

Art Across the Curriculum is a series of activities designed to help you connect the principles of visual art with other subject areas, so students can understand
- that art touches and shapes their lives in ways they might never have imagined,
- and that the arts and sciences are not separate entities.

Art Connections focuses on the basic elements and principles of art, such as line, shape, form, color, emphasis, unity, balance, and texture. *Art Across the Curriculum* works with these basic principles and relates them specifically to **reading/language arts, mathematics, science, social studies,** the other fine arts **(dance, music, theater),** and **technology.**

Each *Art Across the Curriculum* resource book provides a blackline master in each of six curriculum areas for each lesson in the Student Edition of the **Art Connections** program. The lessons are divided into six units of six lessons each, giving you 216 blackline masters for individual and cooperative experiences. Each blackline master is based on curriculum area objectives that are common throughout the country, including those of individual schools, school districts, states, and curriculum area organizations. These objectives are clearly stated at the bottom of each blackline master.

How Do *Art Across the Curriculum* Activities Relate to Art?
The activities in *Art Across the Curriculum* are connected in several ways to the art lessons in **Art Connections.** Often, they extend the specific concept presented in the lesson. For example, geometric figures in art are related directly to geometric figures in mathematics. The activities sometimes spring from the content of the artwork. For instance, Ben Jones's *King Family* is a natural part of a study on Martin Luther King, Jr., and the contributions he and his family have made to our society.

How Do I Use *Art Across the Curriculum?*
The *Art Across the Curriculum* activities are designed to be used in at least two ways:
- to extend the art lesson into other subject areas. In this case, you can review the activities that go with the art lesson and choose one or more to assign. You may use any or all of the blackline masters during your study of a particular element or principle. Generally, you will want to use them in the week in which you present the primary lesson.
- to introduce an art lesson. In this case, you can review the activities in the *Art Across the Curriculum* index in the Teacher Edition to find activities that complement what you are already teaching and introduce the corresponding **Art Connections** lesson through the subject area.

The *Art Across the Curriculum* blackline masters will help you tie basic art principles and elements to all areas of the students' lives.

The Reading/Language Arts Connections

How Do Reading/Language Arts and Visual Art Compare?
The elements and principles of art, such as line, shape, form, color, emphasis, unity, balance, and texture, are also extremely important elements of language. As we write, we endeavor to express our ideas as clearly and precisely as possible. In this attempt, we learn the form, unity, and balance of our language. As we write and speak, we add action, description, and feeling (correlating to line, shape, texture, and color in art) to achieve balance and to create emphasis.

What Do the Reading/Language Arts Activities Cover?
The activities in the reading/language arts category of *Art Across the Curriculum* provide opportunities for using language and extending language experiences while relating to the elements, principles, and subject matter of the art. Through the many activities afforded in these blackline masters, the students will
• develop vocabulary.
• record ideas and feelings.
• develop organizational and writing skills.
• distinguish between fact and opinion.
• use descriptive words.
• become familiar with a variety of genres.
• make comparisons.
• predict outcomes.
• make inferences.
• develop their skills in usage and grammar.
• acquire skills in writing for a variety of purposes.

How Do the Reading/Language Arts Activities Relate to the *Art Connections* Lessons?
The Reading/Language Arts activities are related to the art lessons in a variety of ways:
• the art stimulates writing.
• the art serves as a source for developing vocabulary and literary techniques, such as metaphor, synonyms, compounds, comparison, and exaggeration.
• the art provides ideas for descriptive words.
• the lesson subject matter serves as a springboard for gathering and analyzing information.

The Mathematics Connections

How Do Mathematics and Visual Art Compare?
We often think of mathematics and art as unrelated. However, art is one way to show mathematical principles, and many of the principles of art are mathematical. For example, we can draw pictures of most math problems. In addition, line, shape, and form are an integral part of mathematics.

What Do the Mathematics Activities Cover?
The activities in the mathematics category of *Art Across the Curriculum* cover such skills and concepts as
- patterning,
- critical attributes of geometric shapes and solids,
- number,
- mathematical operations,
- ratio,
- probability,
- graphing,
- measurement,
- problem solving,
- reasoning.

How Do the Mathematics Activities Relate to the *Art Connections* Lessons?
The mathematics activities provided in *Art Across the Curriculum* relate to the art lessons in a variety of ways:
- the art provides opportunities for describing attributes.
- the art serves as a source for identifying geometric shapes and forms.
- the art affords opportunities for problem solving and using mathematical operations.
- the art launches graphing and charting activities.

The Science Connections

How Do Science and Visual Art Compare?

Artists do think like scientists in many ways. They study nature as carefully as scientists—sometimes from the same perspective, sometimes from a different one. When the students are studying a landscape or a still life in **Art Connections,** for example, they must look at the objects scientifically. They will notice that artists are sometimes quite precise and objective in their representation of a natural object or phenomenon; other times artists are more concerned with creating an impression or feeling associated with the natural object. In any case, a good artist uses scientific principles in the work of art.

Art has been a major means of expression and communication since humans have been on Earth. It is likely that art was used before or at least in connection with the development of a language system. We have always used art to describe elements in nature, to record our scientific observations, and to express our ideas and feelings.

Many of the artworks people have created involve nature in some way. Although these portrayals are not always realistic, they are based on scientific reality, our beliefs of reality, and our interpretation of it. Relating science and art is, therefore, a perfect opportunity to develop students' understanding of the connections in our world.

What Do the Science Activities Cover?

The activities included in *Art Across the Curriculum* often spring from the subject of the artwork. Art is a natural way to lead into
- the effects of industry on our environment,
- characteristics of organisms,
- structures of life,
- behavior,
- change,
- properties of matter,
- observation,
- scientific method,
- interpreting and analyzing data,
- the effects of external stimuli on nature, energy, force, and motion.

How Do the Science Activities Relate to the *Art Connections* Lessons?

Many of the science activities spring from examining the artwork. For example,
- the artwork can lead students into the properties of the artists' media.
- the students might examine the plants and animals in an ecosystem depicted in the art.
- Earth science and astronomy activities relate to phenomena exemplified in a work of art.

The Social Studies Connections

How Do Social Studies and Visual Art Compare?
Many of the disciplines of art are also disciplines of the social studies: history and culture, production, perception, criticism, and expression. One of the major goals of many artists is expressing the social issues and the cultures of a society. This is also a primary concern of social scientists. The social scientist is also concerned with emphasis, unity, balance, and harmony as principles that influence the success of a society.

What Do the Social Studies Activities Cover?
The social studies activities in *Art Across the Curriculum* provide opportunities for you to introduce and incorporate many skills and concepts. Some of the objectives covered in these activities include
- mapping, graphing, and charting information,
- economic influences and developments,
- business principles,
- technological development,
- history,
- geography,
- social relationships,
- cultural contributions,
- environmental impact,
- and analyzing and interpreting information.

How Do the Social Studies Activities Relate to the *Art Connections* Lessons?
Because artworks are an expression of culture, the art lesson and the social studies activities are related in a variety of ways:
- the art and the subject matter stimulate the study of a variety of cultures.
- the art and the subject matter serve as a source for developing concepts in history, geography, politics, and sociology.
- the principles and elements of art relate harmony and values to harmony and values in societies and cultures.

The Arts Connections

How Do the Arts and Visual Art Compare?

We generally consider artists to be those who express themselves through art, dance, music, and the theater, so the connections among these areas are more immediately obvious than the connections to other disciplines. The elements and principles of dance, music, and theater are basically the same as those of art—line, shape, form, color, emphasis, unity, balance, and texture.

What Do the Arts Activities Cover?

The arts activities in *Art Across the Curriculum* include a variety of music, dance, and theatrical experiences. For example, students

- transfer spatial patterns from the visual to the kinesthetic,
- develop spatial awareness and control,
- interpret works of art in music, dance, and drama,
- reproduce an artwork dramatically, incorporating scenery, costumes, emotions, and dialogue,
- develop an appreciation of a variety of cultures to all areas of the arts,
- use dance, music, and drama to express feelings and ideas.

How Do the Arts Activities Relate to the *Art Connections* Lessons?

The ties among the arts are quite strong. For example,

- while studying the artist's use of texture in their **Art Connections** lesson, students can easily see the connections to texture in music, dance, and theater. In these areas, texture is developed by variation in style, movement, and intensity.
- artworks will inspire interpretation through music, dance, and theater.
- the subject of a work of art leads to comparable representations in music, song, movement, character, setting, and story.

The Technology Connections

How Do Computer Technology and Visual Art Compare?
The computer opens a new world for artists. Not only is it a new medium for expression, it also gives the artist a different way to combine the elements of art. More and more, we are seeing the computer as a tool for producing, manipulating, and viewing graphics.

What Application Should I Use?
The activities in the technology section of *Art Across the Curriculum* were designed for use with Davidson's **Multimedia Workshop** but will work with most drawing and painting programs. Depending on your computer and software, you will find some minor differences in specifics. For example, the drawing tool on your software might look different than the one used on these blackline masters. We use a wide paintbrush. Your software might use a pencil or a narrow brush. The students will probably adapt to these differences without any difficulty.

What Computer Basics Do Students Need?
Students need at least one introductory computer lesson before they begin any of these activities. They should receive basic instruction on opening, closing, and saving files, as well as clicking and dragging objects. They should become familiar with the basic use of tools and menu commands. Students might need guidance and further instruction during each lesson.

What Do the Technology Activities Cover?
The technology activities provide a wide variety of experiences that encourage students to
- learn the basic techniques for using drawing and painting programs, such as clicking and dragging, copying, pasting, moving, and manipulating.
- discover that there are many ways to accomplish most tasks.
- sketch and draw.
- practice techniques that simulate watercolor, oil, airbrush, and chalk.
- manipulate text and graphs to create multimedia presentations.

The lessons are independent of each other. Students do not need to complete all of the earlier lessons in order to understand instructions in the later lessons. Some of the lessons are shorter than others, so you might want to have students work on more than one lesson in a given session.

How Do the Technology Activities Relate to the *Art Connections* Lessons?
The technology activities give students a different medium for experimenting with the principles and techniques presented in their **Art Connections** lessons. For example,
- the techniques used in the artworks can often be translated to drawing and painting on the computer. There are limitations, however. Forms and texture, for instance, cannot be created on the computer; they can only be represented.
- the subject of a work of art provides an opportunity for students to interpret the subject in their own way.

Name _____ Date _____

UNDERSTANDING WORDS BY THEIR HISTORIES

The lines artists use can be named for the direction of their movement. The words that name lines came into English long ago from other languages. The history of a word often shows that people first used it to compare a thing to something they observed in the natural world.

WHAT TO DO: Match the word describing a line with its history.

curved   from Latin *vertic-*, which means "top of the head, summit"

spiral   from Greek *dia-*, "across, through" + *gonia,* "angle"

vertical   from Latin *spira*, which means "coil"

diagonal   from Latin *curvus*, which means "bent"

straight   from Middle English *strecchen*, which means "to stretch"

horizontal   from Greek *horos*, which means "boundary"

Now, write a sentence explaining each kind of line.

1. A spiral _____

_____

2. A diagonal line _____

_____

3. A vertical line _____

_____

Reading/Language Arts Objective: The student investigates word origins as an aid to understanding meanings as well as historical influences on the English language.

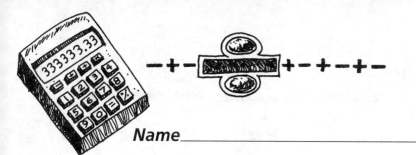

Name_____ Date_____

DIVISION PATTERNS

In art, lines of different kinds are used to create patterns. A weaver, for example, creates pleasing patterns by repeating certain numbers of threads in a certain order.

Designs for fabric can be made by dividing different kinds of lines into sets.

WHAT TO DO: Show how each set of lines below has been divided to form the design on the ribbon. Write the total number of lines in the set, the number of subsets, and the number of lines in each subset. Then write the division problem.

1. total diagonal lines _____

subsets of lines_____

lines in each subset _____

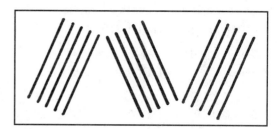

2. total curved lines_____

subsets of lines_____

lines in each subset _____

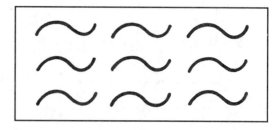

3. total zigzag lines _____

subsets of lines_____

lines in each subset _____

Mathematics Objective: The student describes a pattern to generate the rules of divisibility.

Name _____   Date _____

PLANNING TO RECYCLE

In *Incantation*, Charles Sheeler makes the factory big and powerful.
Industry is important to the United States, which produces and uses
many products. However, industry is eating up our resources. Also,
many factories pollute the water, air, and ground. We need to find
ways to save resources. We can recycle and reuse some resources, such
as paper and plastic. We can reduce the amount of energy and goods
we use.

WHAT TO DO: Pick one resource from the list. Think of three ways to
recycle it, reuse it, or reduce the amount of it you use. List these ways.

water	coal (electricity)	oil (gasoline)
wood (paper)	natural gas (for heat)	plastics
metals (aluminum, steel, tin)		

SCIENCE

1. _____

_____

2. _____

_____

3. _____

_____

How can you help conserve resources best? Make a plan. List how,
where, and when you can do the most. Try to think of something new
and different!

I CAN

_____

_____

Science Objective: The student designs and implements plans for reducing, reusing, and recycling in his or her
community.

Name _____ Date _____

CONTRASTING INDUSTRIAL AND EARLIER CULTURES

The art of a society is like a mirror for its culture. The women who wove the *Huipil* worked by hand, using traditional, ancient patterns. They probably lived in a village, in simple houses, with few belongings. They raised their own food and made their own clothing.

The industrial world of *Incantation* is filled with busy cities, advanced technology, and people who work away from home and who buy what they need. Speed, convenience, and excitement are what these people value.

WHAT TO DO: Read each phrase below. If a phrase describes the life of the weaver, write **weaver** on the line. If a phrase describes the life of a factory worker, write **factory worker** on the line.

_____ paycheck to bank

_____ hunt for and raise own food

_____ hut with no light

_____ house with electric lights

_____ running water

_____ no running water

_____ travel on foot or by horse

_____ trade for needed items

_____ drought a serious problem

_____ wear hand-woven clothing

_____ wear manufactured clothing

_____ buy food in grocery store

_____ crime a serious problem

_____ car or public transportation

Social Studies Objective: The student describes how mass production and the Industrial Revolution affected the economic growth of Texas and the United States.

SOCIAL STUDIES

Name_____   **Date**_____

LINES IN A DANCE

An artist makes lines on a page to create shapes, moods, and movement. A dancer is also drawing invisible lines as he or she dances. To learn a dance, you may study a pattern of lines that shows how to move your feet. In such a diagram, the right foot is shaded, and steps are numbered 1, 2, 3, and so on.

WHAT TO DO: Learn a dance step using lines and simple counting. Study the pattern of lines for the waltz. Practice the steps while counting the beats (1-2-3, 4-5-6).

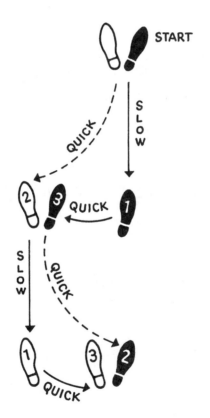

Now, make up your own dance step. On the back of this page, draw the pattern of lines your feet will make as you dance. Using your pattern, teach someone else your dance.

Arts (Dance) Objectives: The student accurately transfers a spatial pattern from the visual to the kinesthetic; The student demonstrates increasing kinesthetic awareness, concentration, and focus in performing movement skills.

Name_____ Date_____

Artists use different kinds of lines to create artwork.

There are five different kinds of lines: vertical, horizontal, diagonal, curved, and zigzag. Lines can be long or short, thick or thin, rough or smooth, or solid or broken.

WHAT TO DO: Draw two pictures using lines.

1. Select the ▦ tool or the ＼ tool. Draw vertical, horizontal, diagonal, curved, and zigzag lines that are:

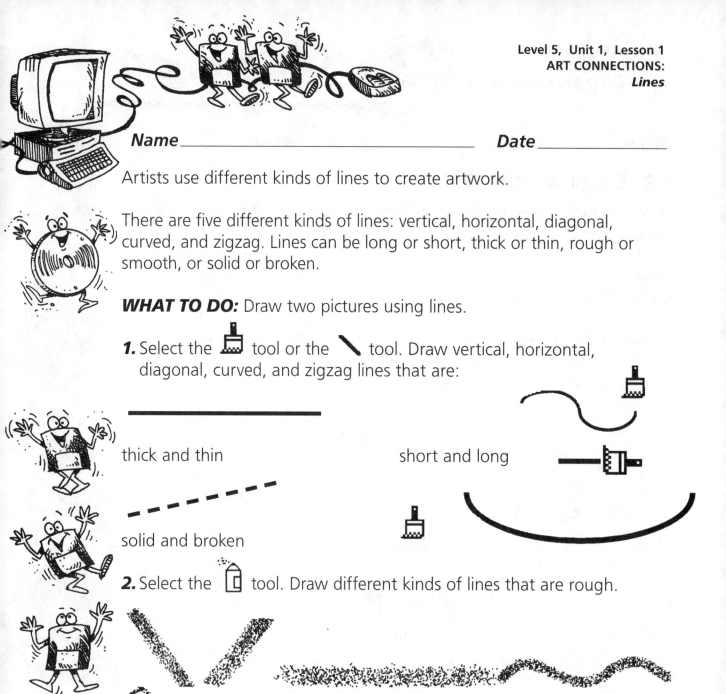

thick and thin   short and long

solid and broken

2. Select the ▯ tool. Draw different kinds of lines that are rough.

3. Draw two pictures using all the different kinds of lines and tools you have explored.

Technology Objective: The student uses software programs with graphics to enhance learning experiences.

6

TECHNOLOGY

LANGUAGE ARTS

Name _____ Date_____

FREE VERSE POETRY

Miró's *Beautiful Bird* uses free-form and geometric shapes imaginatively. His art reminds us of dreams and fantasy, not reality. **Free verse** is a kind of poetry that is free in form. It does not follow a regular beat. It may use rhyme only a little or not at all. Its lines and stanzas may all be different in length.

> *Dark Night*
> *Swirls of light,*
> *Casting shadows across the snowy*
> *landscape*
> *Snowflakes dancing rapidly,*
> *While winds make noise in the night.*

WHAT TO DO: Read the poem again. Think about the word picture it paints. Then answer the questions below.

1. Explain how this poem is different from most poetry you have read.

_____

_____

2. What are the snowflakes doing?

_____

_____

3. What is the poem describing?

_____

_____

Now look again at Miró's painting. On another sheet of paper, write a free-verse poem about the magical bird.

Reading/Language Arts Objective: The student recognizes distinctive features of genres.

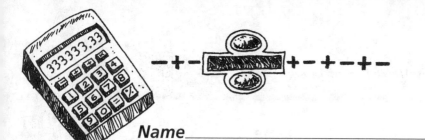

Name_____ Date_____

USING GEOMETRIC SHAPES

Squares, circles, and triangles are three basic geometric shapes. A square has four sides of equal length that meet in four right angles. A triangle has three sides and three angles. A circle is a curved line whose points all lie the same distance from the center. These figures can be combined to create more complex geometric figures.

WHAT TO DO: Identify the geometric shapes used in the picture. Put a star inside each triangle. Shade in each circle with a pencil or crayon. Make an **X** inside each square.

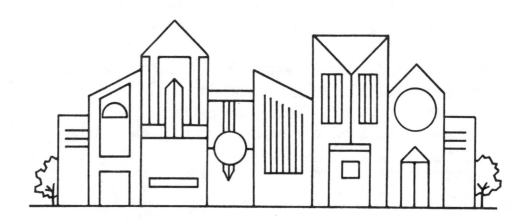

On the back of this paper, draw your own scene using geometric and free-form shapes. Use a ruler and small circle patterns to make straight and curved lines correctly.

Mathematics Objective: The student uses critical attributes to define geometric shapes or solids.

8

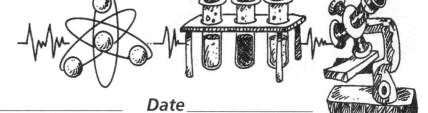

Name_____ Date_____

UNDERSTANDING MIGRATION

Paul Wonner's still-life painting features birds and a field guide to birds. This **field guide** gives many kinds of information about birds, such as their food, nests, and habits of migration. Some birds that **migrate** move from one region to another when the seasons change. They avoid extreme heat and cold and are better able to find food in this way.

WHAT TO DO: Study the following field guide page about robins. Use the information to answer the questions below.

ROBIN
A common bird often seen on lawns searching for insects and earthworms. In cold weather prefers woods or fruit-bearing trees. Builds a nest of grass and mud in orchard trees or shrubs or on buildings. Migrates in flocks by day.

1. In fall, what will the robins do who passed the summer in Canada?

_____

2. In spring, what will the robins do who passed the winter in Mexico?

_____

3. In which two countries would you find robins' nests in spring?

_____

4. What summer food does a robin hunt in a yard in the northern United States? _____

_____

5. Why don't robins rely on this food in winter?_____

_____

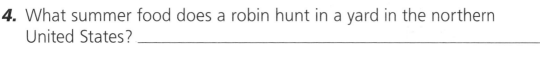

Science Objective: The student interprets and describes the behavioral changes in organisms resulting from external stimuli.

9

Name_____ Date_____

USING SHAPES TO GRAPH FACTS

In art, shape is the basis for meaning. In maps and graphs, shape is used to make information easier to understand. The **circle graph** below shows you how land in the United States is used. The **bar graph** compares the areas of the Great Lakes. What shapes have been used?

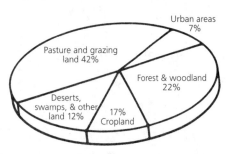

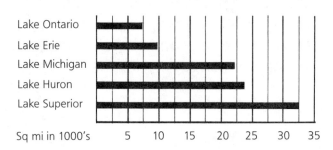

WHAT TO DO: Create two graphs to show the information below. Sketch your ideas on this page. Then, draw your graphs neatly on a new sheet of paper.

1. Make a bar graph to compare the longest rivers in the world.

Nile, Africa	4,000 miles
Amazon, South America	3,900 miles
Yangtze, China	3,100 miles
Mississippi, U.S.A.	2,500 miles

2. Make a circle graph to show how a city gets money.
[HINT: 25% = $\frac{1}{4}$; 50% = $\frac{1}{2}$; 10% = $\frac{1}{10}$.]

Sources of Income	Percent
Sales and utility taxes	25 %
Property tax	50 %
State income tax	20 %
Other (fines, fees, special services, and so on)	5 %

Social Studies Objective: The student creates geographic tools such as maps, charts, and graphs.

SOCIAL STUDIES

Name _____ Date _____

WRITING A SONG

Miró's painting shows an amazing event: a beautiful bird tells an important secret to two people in love. For centuries, people have listened to birds' songs with pleasure and interest. They have created songs for instruments and voices that imitate birds' songs.

WHAT TO DO: Imagine you are the magical bird of the Miró painting. You are singing your secret to the people in the painting. Invent the words and melody for your song.

1. What is your secret? Write it as the words for a song.

_____

_____

2. Decide what the song will be like to create the mood you want.
   a. The mood is _____.
   b. The tempo is (fast or slow) _____.
   c. The kind of voice is (high, deep) _____.
   d. The instruments that make the right type of sounds are

violin	flute	clarinet
guitar	drum	trumpet
saxophone	bass	piano (or keyboard)

   other _____
   e. The meter should be (four even beats, three quick beats, and so on)

   _____.

3. Songs have a melody, or tune, that repeats. Invent a melody for your song.

4. Practice your song, putting the words and melody together with the beat and tempo. If you have an instrument, use it, but your voice alone is fine. Make any changes you want. Perform the song for family or classmates.

THE ARTS

Arts (Music) Objectives: The student improvises short melodies in a consistent style, meter, and tonality; The student compares in two or more arts how the characteristic materials of each art can be used to transform similar events into works of art.

Name _____ Date _____

Shapes can be geometric or free-form. Squares, circles, and triangles are basic geometric shapes. Uneven and irregular shapes are free-form shapes.

WHAT TO DO: Draw a picture using geometric and free-form shapes.

1. Select the ▭ and ⬯ shape tools. Click + and drag to draw several geometric shapes.

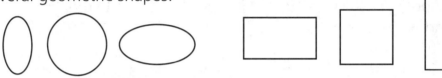

2. Select the ╲ tool. Draw triangles.

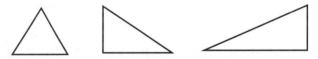

3. Combine basic geometric shapes to create complex geometric shapes.

Move a shape by selecting it with the ◌ tool and dragging it to another place on the screen.

Rotate a shape by selecting it with the ⬚ tool and choosing a command from the Selection menu.

4. Select the 🖌 tool or the ✏ tool. Draw free-form shapes.

5. Draw a picture using geometric and free-form shapes. Overlap the shapes.

Technology Objective: The student uses software programs with graphics to enhance learning experiences.

TECHNOLOGY

Name _____ **Date** _____

EXPLAINING A PARADOX

M. C. Escher and Wendy Fay Dixon created optical illusions or visual tricks in their works. A writer creates a **paradox,** a statement that seems to contradict itself but actually has truth to it. For example, "A thundering silence followed her announcement" has the words **thundering** and **silence.** Thundering is a very loud sound. Silence means no sound at all. Using the two words together tells us that her announcement surprised everyone so much that everyone "sounded loud" but did not say a word. A paradox emphasizes or attracts attention to an idea.

WHAT TO DO: Choose a paradox from the list. Write a paragraph explaining what makes it seem impossible or false and why it could be true.

1. Parting is such sweet sorrow.
2. The climber felt the ice burning into his bare hands.
3. The dog is more intelligent than the rabbit.
4. No news is good news.

_____

_____

_____

_____

_____

_____

Reading/Language Arts Objectives: The student uses writing as a tool for reflection, exploration, problem solving, and personal growth; The student writes to inform.

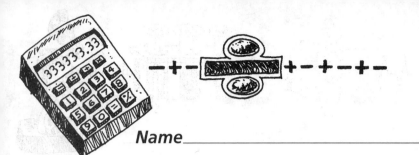

Name_____ Date_____

RATIOS

To make an area darker, artists use more dark lines, dots, or other shapes in that area. The more shading in an area, the darker the value. In other words, the higher the proportion of dots or lines in an area, the darker the value.

In math, we call a proportion a **ratio.** A ratio shows the relationship of one thing to another in the form of a number.

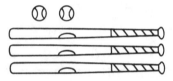  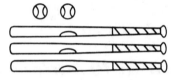

The ratio of balls to baseball bats is 2 to 3, or $\frac{2}{3}$ (a fraction). This means that for every two baseballs, there are three bats.

WHAT TO DO: Study the proportions of things below. Find the ratios of shaded squares of different values.

1. Write the fraction that shows the ratio of
   a. black squares to total squares   _____   _____
   b. black squares to white squares   _____   _____
   c. gray squares to white squares   _____   _____
   d. white squares to all other squares _____   _____

2. For each shape, write the ratio of black to white.
   Circle: _____   Kite: _____

Mathematics Objective: The student uses fractions as a way to represent the concept of ratio.

Name _____ *Date* _____

UNDERSTANDING NEEDS FOR SURVIVAL

Deidre surprises us because the girl appears to be underwater. People cannot live underwater as fish can. Different living things have different ways of getting what they need to survive. They must get food, air, light, and water from their environment. They must also be able to get rid of wastes.

WHAT TO DO: Fill in the chart to show how each living thing gets what it needs to live.

Needs	Fish	People
air		
food		
water		

SCIENCE

Now, imagine life on the imaginary planet Xeno. It has an atmosphere of carbon dioxide. The entire surface of the planet is ice, and the sun shines two hours a day. Plants are microscopic, and they live in the ice. Invent an animal that lives on Xeno. Tell what it needs to survive and how it meets its needs. On the back of the page, draw a picture of the animal.

_____

_____

_____

_____

_____

_____

Science Objective: The student creates a make-believe organism that has characteristics and structures appropriate for life in a given ecosystem.

Name_____ Date_____

PURPOSES OF POLITICAL PARTIES

The word **value** can have different meanings. Value in art means lightness or darkness. To a nation, values are ideals or principles that are important. One way we protect our values is to vote for candidates who share our values.

WHAT TO DO: Read the paragraph about political parties. Then answer the questions.

Political parties are groups of people working together to elect government leaders. They are necessary in a democracy for several reasons. First, they provide platforms made up of ideas and solutions to problems. Second, political parties provide a means for selecting our lawmakers, president, and vice-president. Third, political parties provide balance and help avoid abuses of political power.

PURPOSES OF POLITICAL PARTIES:

1. Why were political parties formed?

_____

_____

2. What is one purpose or goal of political parties?

_____

_____

3. What do you know about political parties in local elections?

_____

_____

Social Studies Objective: The student explains why political parties were formed.

16

SOCIAL STUDIES

Name_____ Date_____

CREATING ILLUSION ONSTAGE

In the painting *Deidre*, light and dark create the illusion that Deidre is underwater, peering through the fish swimming past. In drama, lighting is also used to make someone or something appear to be what it is not. Costumes, scenery, props (such as furniture), and makeup complete the illusion. For example, a soft blue light shining on an actor dressed in a flowing ruffled outfit can help us believe she is a ballerina onstage.

WHAT TO DO: Decide who Deidre is, where she is, and what she is doing. Plan her story as a fantasy play. Then create just the right stage set. Fill in details for each of the four areas below. In the oval "stage," draw some scenery and props or the costume you have invented.

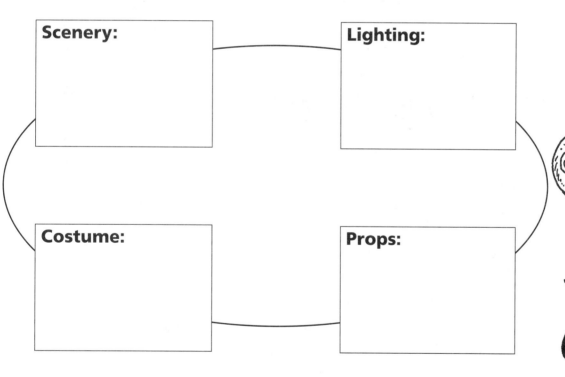

Scenery:

Lighting:

Costume:

Props:

THE ARTS

Arts (Theater) Objective: The student works collaboratively and safely to select and create elements of scenery, props, lighting, and sound to signify environments, and costumes and makeup to suggest character.

Name_____ Date_____

Value is the lightness and darkness of a color or object. Shading is used to darken values by adding black or repeating several lines close together.

WHAT TO DO: Show value in drawings of a three-dimensional object from different viewpoints.

1. Select the ☐ shape tool. Click + and drag. Create two rows of seven boxes each.

☐☐☐☐☐☐☐

2. Use the ✍ tool to create a value scale in the first row. Fill each box with a different pattern to create values going from light to dark.

3. Use the ⬚ tool to create a value scale in the second row. Fill each box with a different value going from light to dark.

4. Choose a three-dimensional object to draw. Use the ✐ tool or the 🖌 tool to draw the object from different points of view.

5. Use the ✐ tool or the ⬚ tool to add value to the drawings with shading.

Technology Objective: The student uses software programs with graphics to enhance learning experiences.

TECHNOLOGY

LANGUAGE ARTS

Name _____ Date_____

WRITING TO EXPRESS EMOTION

Sharecropper and *The Downtrodden* express great sadness and weariness. Poverty and a hard life have marked the people in these artworks.

Emotions can be expressed in writing also. Journals, letters, and poems can all be used by writers to record feelings for different audiences. Many people keep a **journal,** which is a private record of experiences and feelings. To share feelings, we write **letters** to friends and family. **Poems** share deep emotions with the world.

WHAT TO DO: Imagine you are a person in Catlett's or Köllwitz's artwork. Write a journal entry, letter, or poem that expresses your feelings. Be sure to include details about your life.

_____

_____

_____

_____

_____

_____

_____

Reading/Language Arts Objectives: The student writes to express emotions, to develop and record ideas, and to reflect; The student chooses the appropriate form for his or her purpose for writing.

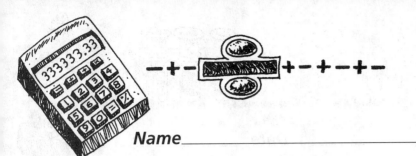

Name_____   Date_____

USING ORDERED PAIRS TO LOCATE REGIONS

Parallel lines are used to create value in artwork. The number and closeness of lines placed side by side determine the darkness of areas. Parallel lines are also used to make a grid.

The numbers on the sides give each point on the grid an address. For example, the triangle below has corners at (1,1), at (2,3), and at (3,1). These pairs of numbers are called **ordered pairs.** The two numbers in an ordered pair are called **coordinates.** The first coordinate in each pair tells the location on the horizontal number line, and the second coordinate tells the location on the vertical number line. The two coordinates together identify a point on the grid.

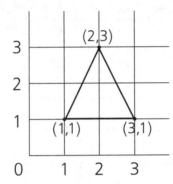

WHAT TO DO: Study the figure on the grid below. Then, write the coordinates of each point.

a. _____

b. _____

c. _____

d. _____

e. _____

f. _____

g. _____

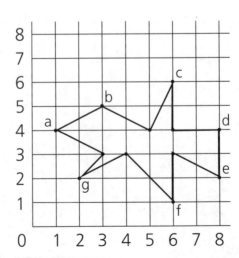

Mathematics Objective: The student uses ordered pairs of whole numbers to locate or name points on a coordinate grid.

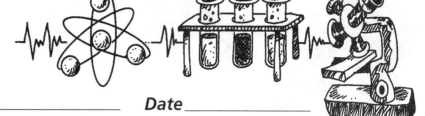

Name _____   Date _____

INVESTIGATING VALUE

How are dark values achieved in an artwork? If the same width and type of lines are used to create values, you can analyze, or figure out, exactly what makes each step in the value scale.

WHAT TO DO: Design a method to determine how each level of darkness in the value scale is created. Use the method outlined in steps 1 to 5.

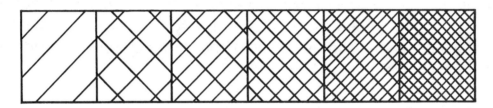

Experimental method:

1. State the problem to be solved: _____

_____

2. Gather information (number and slant of lines in each step in the scale):
Step A _____ / _____ \   Step D _____ / _____ \
Step B _____ / _____ \   Step E _____ / _____ \
Step C _____ / _____ \   Step F _____ / _____ \

3. Try to figure it out: Each step in the value scale is created by

_____

4. Try it out. Test your idea by creating your own value scale using the same method.

5. Evaluate and conclude. Did your experiment work? Is your idea right? What would you do differently next time? My conclusion is that

_____

_____

Science Objective: The student designs and conducts an appropriate investigation to answer a given question.

Name _____ Date _____

SHARECROPPING AND THE SOUTHERN ECONOMY

Catlett's sharecropper was a farmer. Before the Civil War, African Americans worked for landowners to produce cotton and tobacco. After 1865, they were freed but did not have resources to farm for themselves. Many became sharecroppers. They rented land, housing, and equipment from landowners. They were given a small amount of the profit from the crops they produced.

For many, life as a sharecropper was not easy. Today, machines have made farming more of a big business and a science. Sharecroppers have almost disappeared. Landowners work the land themselves, and do not need many workers.

WHAT TO DO: Finish the timetable by writing the letters of the captions in the correct boxes.

A. Farmers use machinery to plant and harvest.
B. Plantations use African Americans as laborers.
C. Landowners rent to sharecroppers.

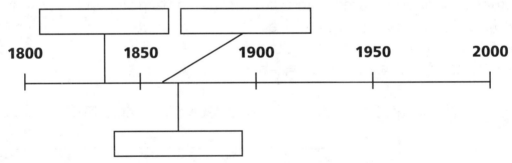

Find out about farming in the South a hundred years ago and today. On a separate sheet of paper, write a short report about people and machines.

Social Studies Objectives: The student researches an area of development such as agriculture and illustrates the major changes during a selected period of time; The student evaluates effects of supply and demand on economic activities such as demand for cotton and its effect on plantation owners and slaves.

Name _____ Date _____

UNDERSTANDING SPIRITUALS

Spirituals are a type of religious song developed by African Americans. They began as group songs. A verse sung by a leader was answered by a chorus. Spirituals were sung at work and at religious meetings. The strong beat was often emphasized by clapping. "Swing Low, Sweet Chariot," "Deep River," and "Nobody Knows the Trouble I've Seen" are among the best-known spirituals.

WHAT TO DO: Use the information to answer the questions.

1. What kind of emotion do you think most spirituals express? Why?

_____

2. Here are some of the words for "Swing Low, Sweet Chariot." Explain what you think they meant to the people who originally sang them.

*I looked over Jordan and what did I see
(coming for to carry me home)?
A band of angels coming after me
(coming for to carry me home).
Swing low, sweet chariot
Coming for to carry me home.*

_____

_____

_____

3. Circle the phrases that best describe spirituals.

repetition	accompanied by many instruments
strong rhythm	solo and chorus refrain
accented by gestures	complex melody
clear, strong emotion	

THE ARTS

Arts (Music) Objective: The student describes distinguishing characteristics of representative music genres and styles from a variety of cultures.

Name_____   Date_____

Line patterns create different values.

WHAT TO DO: Create light and dark values in drawings.

1. Select the ☐ shape tool. Click + and drag. Create five boxes.

2. Select the ＼ tool and a line thickness. Draw repeated parallel lines in each box to create value. Use thin lines that are far apart and thick lines that are close together. Make a value scale with lines.

3. Draw simple objects using the ☐ or ⬭ shape tool or the ✏ tool or the 🖌 tool.

4. Use the ＼ tool or the ✏ tool to add parallel lines to the objects to create light and dark values.

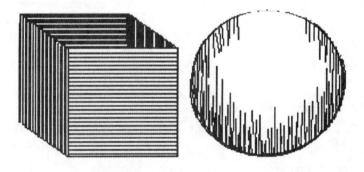

Technology Objective: The student uses software programs with graphics to enhance learning experiences.

Name _____ Date _____

A UNIFIED COMPOSITION

Jesse Treviño has arranged the people in *Mis Hermanos* to show they belong together. His composition has **unity.** Good compositions or paragraphs also have unity. The ideas are organized in **logical order** and are often connected to one another with **transitional phrases** such as "as a result," "for example," "first (or next)," or "in spite of this."

WHAT TO DO: The sentences below could describe the people in *Mis Hermanos*. Number them to show the most logical order for a paragraph.

_____ Brothers, sisters, cousins, aunts, and uncles gather at my grandparents' house in San Antonio.

_____ The next day everyone packs picnic baskets and heads for the park.

_____ The first day everyone chatters and cooks and catches up on news.

_____ It is noisy and confusing and hard to hear.

_____ The annual reunion of the Ramirez family is two days of nonstop fun.

_____ No one would change it, and everyone looks forward to the next reunion.

_____ No one minds the confusion because we are so glad to see one another.

_____ Everyone enjoys games, dancing, and swimming.

_____ Everyone eats too much and is very tired by the end of the day.

On another sheet of paper, write the paragraph with the sentences in order. Add transitions to tie the sentences together.

Reading/Language Arts Objective: The student produces cohesive written forms (for example, by organizing ideas, smoothing transitions, using precise wording).

Name_____ Date_____

FINDING VOLUME

In drawing, shading creates the illusion of depth. The shaded object appears to be solid. Solid objects have three dimensions: length, width, and depth. **Volume** is the measure of the space taken up by a solid figure. To find the volume of a figure, multiply width by length by depth (or height).

A cube with two-inch sides has a volume of eight cubic inches.

2 inches ✕ 2 inches ✕ 2 inches = 8 cubic inches

WHAT TO DO: Circle each object that has three dimensions. Find the volume of each figure. Write the volume on the line.

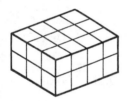

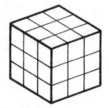

_____ _____

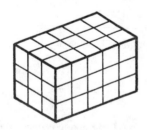

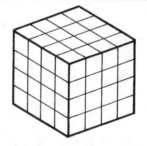

_____ _____

Find a box or other solid figure and measure the object. On the back of this page, draw a picture and show how you calculated the volume.

Mathematics Objectives: The student measures volume using concrete models of cubic units.

26

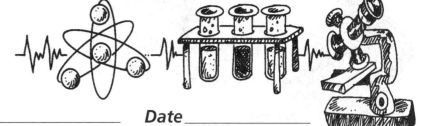

Name _____ Date _____

REFLECTED LIGHT AND MIRRORS

The bright areas in *Mis Hermanos* and *Two Young Girls* are areas where light is reflected. Light waves that strike an object and bounce back are said to be **reflected**. The type of surface the light hits determines the type of reflection that is formed.

WHAT TO DO: Study the diagrams of reflected light. Answer the questions.

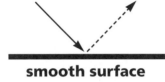

smooth surface

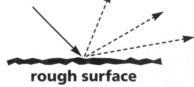

rough surface

1. How are light rays reflected when they strike a smooth surface?

_____

_____

2. How are the reflected rays different when they strike a rough, or irregular, surface?

_____

_____

3. Which diagram shows light reflection that will form an image just like the object?_____

4. Which diagram shows light reflection that will form a fuzzy image?_____

5. Light rays bounce off a mirror at an angle equal but opposite to the angle at which they strike it. How could you use mirrors and cardboard to make a **periscope** (an instrument for seeing around corners)? Draw your plan on the back of this sheet.

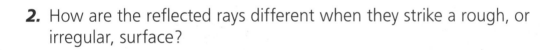

Science Objective: The student uses mirrors and lenses to construct optical devices.

SCIENCE

Name _____ Date _____

USING MAPS TO LEARN HISTORY

The Hispanic men in Jesse Treviño's painting share a Mexican ancestry. One-fourth of the population of Texas is Mexican American. The history of Texas shows why. Changing boundaries play an important role in Texas history. **Political maps** show how the boundaries of Texas have changed over time.

WHAT TO DO: Study the political maps of what is now Texas to answer the questions below.

Red River

Rio Grande River

Spanish Territory

1700s–1823

Republic of Texas

1836–1845

New Mexico

Oklahoma

Arkansas
Louisiana

State of Texas

1845 to present

1. Write the name of the country that controlled the Texas territory in the blank beside each date:

   a. 1820 _____ **b.** 1846 _____

2. What rivers form part of the boundaries of Texas?

   _____

3. Name the states that border Texas.

   _____

   _____

Social Studies Objective: The student uses geographic tools such as maps, atlases, charts, and graphs to organize, interpret, and share information about people, places, events, and the environment.

SOCIAL STUDIES

Name _____ **Date** _____

MUSIC CULTURE THEN AND NOW

The girls in Renoir's painting are playing a piece on the piano. They were about your age a hundred years ago. Like piano students today, they played music by composers such as Beethoven, Mozart, Chopin, and Brahms. Playing for family and friends was a common entertainment. Playing well was an admired skill–performing for small gatherings added pleasure, relaxation, and refinement to a home. The girls may have practiced several hours a day.

WHAT TO DO: Compare your entertainment with those of the girls in the painting. Answer the questions to show how music and entertainment then and now are alike and different.

1. List ways you enjoy playing or listening to music. Tell how they are the same and how they are different from what the girls in the painting would have done.

_____

_____

2. What instrument do you play or would you like to learn to play? Why, when, and where would you play it?

_____

_____

3. How and where do people listen to music today? How does this compare to a hundred years ago?

_____

_____

4. What other entertainment do you enjoy? Explain how the entertainment may be different from someone your age of a hundred years ago.

_____

_____

THE ARTS

Arts (Music) Objective: The student compares, in several cultures, functions music serves, roles of musicians, and conditions under which music is typically performed.

Name_____ Date_____

The darkness or lightness of an object is described by its value. Value is shown with shadows and highlights. Shadows are the shaded area in a drawing. Highlights are the brightest spots of a drawing.

WHAT TO DO: Show highlights and shadows in a drawing of a classmate.

1. Select the ✏ tool or the 🖌 tool. Sketch a piece of draped fabric.

2. Use the 🖍 tool to add shadows.

3. Use the ⬱ tool to add highlights or white areas.

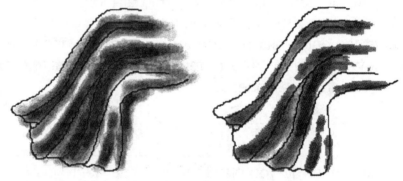

4. Create a shaded drawing of a class member. Use a lamp or strong light source to create highlights and shadows. Use the ✏ tool, the 🖌 tool, and the 🖍 tool.

Technology Objective: The student uses software programs with graphics to enhance learning experiences.

TECHNOLOGY

Name _____ Date_____

CREATING INTEREST AND VARIETY IN SENTENCES

There are many contrasts in *Boy and Car*, *New York City* and *American Rural Baroque*. One has more light and one more dark. One has more solid, heavy lines and one more delicate, swirly ones. One is in the city; the other is in the country.

To make writing more interesting, you can set up contrasts. Make your sentences different in length and structure. Use some questions and exclamations in addition to statements. Combine opposite ideas using **but** or **yet**. (For example, "I liked seeing the countryside, but I hated having to sit still for so long.")

WHAT TO DO: Imagine you are the little boy in *Boy and Car*, *New York City* photograph. Write about where you are going and what you will see happen when you get there. Use different lengths and kinds of sentences. Use contrasting ideas.

_____

_____

_____

_____

_____

_____

_____

_____

Reading/Language Arts Objectives: The student writes in complete sentences, varying sentence structure as appropriate to meaning and audience. The student writes to entertain self and others.

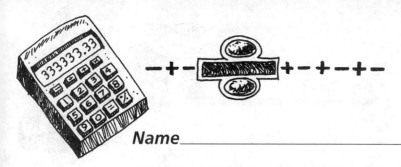

Name_____ Date_____

MEASURING TO CREATE A PATTERN

Study the shadow of the chair in Steiner's photograph. Its contrast to the wall makes it interesting. Even more interesting is the jagged edge of the shadow on the wall of the house. This jagged edge makes a pattern that repeats the chair but gives it a different personality and feeling.

WHAT TO DO: With a ruler, draw a pattern in the first box, using lines, squares, and other interesting geometric shapes. Then draw the same pattern in the second box, using the same measurements for each piece of the pattern.

Mathematics Objective: The student uses measurement procedures to solve problems involving length, weight, etc.

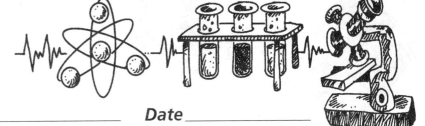

Name _____   Date _____

MASS, FORCE, AND MOVEMENT

The chair, the boy, and the car in the photographs are still. However, they can all be set in motion if a force is applied to them. A **force** is a push or a pull that makes an object move, stop, or change speed or direction.

Mass can be measured in kilograms (kg). A car that weighs 1,000 kilograms is 400 times heavier than a chair that weighs 25 kilograms. It will take 400 times more force to move the car than the chair.

WHAT TO DO: Circle the object in each pair that will require more force to move. In the blank, write how many times more force it will take to move the object with greater mass.

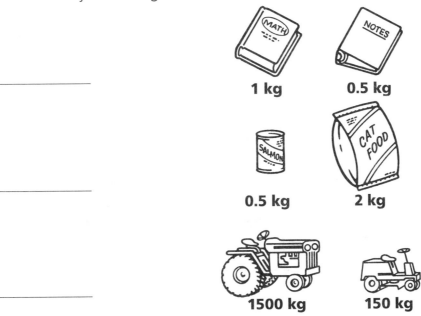

1 kg	**0.5 kg**
0.5 kg	**2 kg**
1500 kg	**150 kg**

_____

_____

_____

Now, plan a way to use the materials pictured below to show that the greater the force, the more the object moves. Write your plan on the back of this page. Illustrate with diagrams and arrows. Demonstrate your plan for someone.

SCIENCE

Science Objective: The student creates a demonstration which explains the motion of objects as a result of the force applied.

Name_____   Date_____

TECHNOLOGY AND THE AUTOMOBILE

Does the car in *Boy and Car, New York City* look odd to you? Since automobiles first appeared in the 1890s, they have changed tremendously. The car in this photograph, built in the 1930s, was much faster, safer, and more comfortable than early cars. Our cars today are still faster, safer, and more comfortable than cars like the one in the photograph. Advances in technology have brought many improvements to our lives.

WHAT TO DO: Write each describing phrase under the appropriate heading. You may need to research if you are not sure.

120 mph speeds
seat belts & air bags
fewer than 500,000 cars in America
more people have cars than do not
automatic ignition
eight-cylinder engines
antilock braking system
synthetic rubber tires
computerized controls

20 mph speeds
high-beam headlights
60 mph speeds
disk brakes
hand brakes
two-cylinder engines
natural rubber tires
radial tires
hand crank to start

1900	1950	NOW

How will cars of the future be different? What advances in technology will change them? Explain your car of the future on the back of this paper. You might want to draw a picture.

Social Studies Objective: The student predicts changes that may occur in the future as a result of new technology.

SOCIAL STUDIES

Name _____   Date _____

THE STAGE

The chair on the porch in *American Rural Baroque* has a dramatic feel that suggests a stage. A bare scene is set, waiting for a character to come onstage and take a seat. What kind of character would you expect to find in this setting? The setting and the character should reinforce each other, or go together well, in a drama.

WHAT TO DO: Decide what drama will be acted out on the porch. Answer the questions below to show how the setting and the character match.

1. Describe the character who sits in the chair.

Name _____

Age _____

Description _____

_____

Personality _____

_____

2. How does your character feel about the chair?

_____

_____

3. How does the setting reinforce your character?

_____

_____

4. Every drama has a conflict. What problem does the character have to

solve? _____

_____

Arts (Theater) Objective: Students explain the functions and interrelated nature of scenery, properties, lighting, etc., in creating an environment appropriate for the drama.

THE ARTS

Name_____ Date_____

Hatching, cross-hatching, and stippling are shading techniques used by artists to create value contrast in drawings.

WHAT TO DO: Draw a shape picture using shading techniques to create value contrast.

1. Select the ☐ shape tool and draw three boxes. Use the ＼ tool, the ✐ tool, and the 🖌 tool to create value contrast in each box. Use different shading techniques:

hatching	cross-hatching	stippling

2. Select the ◯ shape tool and draw three circles. Add shading to each circle using the same techniques as above.

  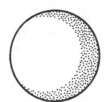 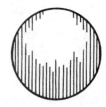

3. Draw a picture using different shapes. Add shading to create value contrast.

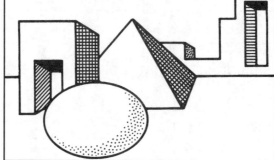

Technology Objective: The student uses software programs with graphics to enhance learning experiences.

TECHNOLOGY

Name _____ Date _____

BIOGRAPHY

Martin Luther King, Jr., whose family is featured in the painting, was a great leader. He inspired many people to protest peacefully for civil rights. Memorable people's lives are recorded by writers in **biographies.** A good biography gives facts about a person and explains why that person was important. Finally, it gives a realistic description of the person.

WHAT TO DO: Imagine that you are writing a biography of Martin Luther King, Jr. Decide what information you will include and where you will get it.

1. What facts about King's early life will you want to include?

_____

_____

2. What facts about his work will you need?

_____

_____

3. Where will you find the information you need?

_____

_____

4. King died in 1968. Whom could you interview to find out more

about him? _____

_____

5. How will you learn what kind of a person King was? What would

give you a sense of what he was really like? _____

_____

Language Arts Objectives: The student generates ideas and plans for writing. The student recognizes distinctive features of genres (for example, biography).

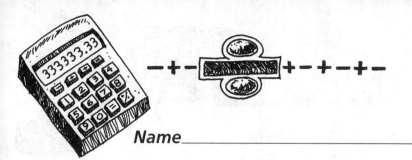

Name_____ Date_____

CALCULATING DISTANCES ON A MAP

Jasper Johns's *Map* emphasizes the states of our country. Every year, millions of Americans travel by car to different states. An important part of trip planning is knowing distances between places.

WHAT TO DO: Use the map and the mileage chart to solve the problems. Show your work in the margin.

Dallas to Chicago............921 miles	
Chicago to New York......809 miles	
New York to	
Washington, DC.......237 miles	
Washington, DC	
to Atlanta.................618 miles	
Atlanta to Dallas............822 miles	

Anna and Mike are traveling from Dallas to Chicago, New York, Washington, DC, and Atlanta.

1. They drive 537 miles the first day. How many miles are they from

Chicago? _____

2. When they reach New York City, how many miles will they have

traveled? _____

3. How many miles must they travel to return to Dallas from Atlanta?

_____

4. How many miles will they travel on the round-trip? _____

Mathematics Objectives: The student selects and uses addition and subtraction strategies, algorithms, and technology to solve problems involving whole numbers and decimals.

Name _____ **Date** _____

SOLVING A MAP-MAKING PROBLEM

Jasper Johns's *Map* combines two techniques: collage and encaustic painting. He applied colors in wax to the surface of the painting using hot irons. The hot wax is flowed like paint, then cooled quickly to a solid form. Many materials have been used in unusual ways to create art.

WHAT TO DO: Use what you know about the properties of materials to help you create a map. Decide how to make a map without using paper or pencils. List materials and tools you will need. Describe the steps you will follow to make the map.

MATERIALS I NEED:

_____

_____

_____

_____

_____

TOOLS I NEED:

_____

_____

_____

STEPS TO MAKE THE MAP:

_____

_____

_____

_____

_____

Science Objective: The student applies his or her knowledge of the properties of matter to solve a design problem.

Name _____ Date _____

RESEARCHING MARTIN LUTHER KING, JR.

The artwork by Ben Jones honors Martin Luther King, Jr., and his family. King did a great deal to advance civil rights in the United States. A Baptist minister, he lead African Americans struggling for equal treatment. King showed a nation that nonviolent protest against injustice was effective.

WHAT TO DO: Read about some of King's achievements. Answer the questions. Then, do research to find out more about King and his work.

1955	1957	1960s	1964	1965
led boycott of bus system in Montgomery, Alabama, to protest unequal treatment of riders	helped found Southern Christian Leadership Conference, an effective civil rights organization	led campaigns for better education and housing for African Americans living in poverty	received the Nobel Peace Prize for leadership of nonviolent struggle for equality in the United States	led major campaign for African-American voter registration in the South

SOCIAL STUDIES

1. Write four questions you want to answer in your research about King.

_____

_____

_____

_____

2. Take notes as you do your research. Use the notes to make a poster, a poem, or a report about King.

Social Studies Objective: The student researches and presents information on a leader from a specific time period.

Name _____ Date _____

SONGS THAT CELEBRATE YOUR STATE

Jasper Johns's *Map* shows us both the unity and variety of the United States. Many songs celebrate qualities of each of the 50 states. Our national anthem celebrates the flag, the best-known symbol of our country.

Francis Scott Key wrote "The Star-Spangled Banner" during a battle of the War of 1812. After the battle, Key was proud to see his country's flag still flying.

WHAT TO DO: Read the words to the first stanza of "The Star-Spangled Banner." Think of other songs you know about the United States, such as "America the Beautiful" or "America." Then, answer the questions.

> Oh, say, can you see, by the dawn's early light,
> What so proudly we hailed at the twilight's last gleaming,
> Whose broad stripes and bright stars, through the perilous fight,
> O'er the ramparts we watched were so gallantly streaming?
> And the rocket's red glare, the bombs bursting in air,
> Gave proof through the night that our flag was still there.
> Oh, say, does that Star-Spangled Banner yet wave
> O'er the land of the free and the home of the brave?

1. What feelings do these patriotic songs show? Write three of the feelings on the lines.

_____

_____

2. Choose one of the feelings you listed. On the back of this page, write a new verse to the tune of "America the Beautiful," "America," or "The Star-Spangled Banner."

3. Sing your song for a friend or for the class.

Arts (Music) Objective: The student sings music representing diverse genres and cultures, with expression appropriate for the work being performed.

Name _____ Date _____

Artists use monochromatic colors to create unity so all of the shapes and forms in their artwork look like they belong together. A monochromatic color scheme uses only one hue and the tints and shades of that hue.

WHAT TO DO: Create six design motifs filled with monochromatic colors.

1. Select the ☐ shape tool and draw a box.
2. Use the ➘ tool and the ☐ and ○ shape tools to add lines and shapes to create a design motif.

3. Select your motif with the ⊏⊐ tool and choose the Copy and Paste commands from the Edit menu to create five more motifs. Choose a command from the Selection menu to flip or rotate a selected motif.

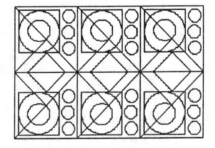

4. Select the ✍ tool and fill each motif with the tints and shades of one primary or secondary color.

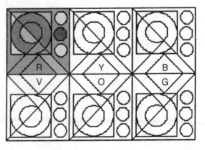

Technology Objective: The student uses software programs with graphics to enhance learning experiences.

TECHNOLOGY

Name _____ Date _____

DESCRIBING A PAINTING

The placement of the stones and jawbone in *Red and Pink Rocks and Teeth* is precise. Exact location, color, and texture of the objects give interest, mood, and meaning. Precise writing demands exact description. When you describe a scene, you use words to help your reader imagine the look, feel, and location of objects in the scene.

WHAT TO DO: Complete the description of O'Keeffe's painting. Choose words that create an exact picture in your reader's mind. Consider these properties of each object:

location   color   size   shape

A large, smooth pink stone with an egg shape sits in the center of the top two-thirds of the picture.

_____

_____

_____

_____

_____

_____

What mood is created by these objects and the way they are combined?

_____

_____

_____

Language Arts Objectives: The student writes to inform (describe). The student analyzes the various ways visual image makers represent meanings.

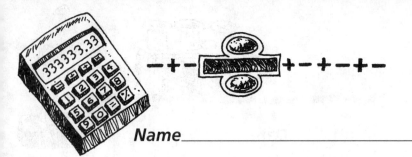

Name_____ Date_____

ADDING DECIMALS

Analogous colors share a common color. Yellow, yellow-green, green, and blue-green are analogous because they all contain yellow. Analogous colors are all lined up together on the color wheel. To add decimals, you have to line them up correctly.

WHAT TO DO: Look at the abstract design. Use information in the design and what you know about analogous colors to solve the problems.

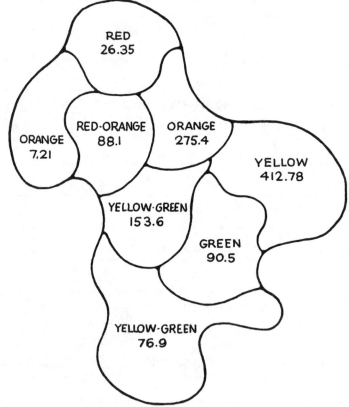

RED
26.35

RED-ORANGE
88.1

ORANGE
275.4

ORANGE
7.21

YELLOW
412.78

YELLOW-GREEN
153.6

GREEN
90.5

YELLOW-GREEN
76.9

1. Find the sum of red and its analogous colors. _____

2. Find the sum of yellow and its analogous colors. _____

3. Which is greater, the total for the shapes that contain yellow and its analogous colors or the total for the shapes that contain red and its

analogous colors? _____

Mathematics Objective: The student selects and uses addition strategies, algorithms, and technology to solve problems involving whole numbers and decimals.

Name _____   Date _____

MAKING A LOOM AND A WEAVING

The *Eye Dazzler* weaving was made on a loom. One kind of Navajo loom is small and portable. Look at the diagram of a weaving closely. Can you see how the horizontal threads are woven in and out through vertical strands?

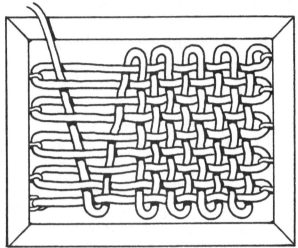

WHAT TO DO: Find the materials listed below. Solve the problem of how to put them together to make a simple loom.

POSSIBLE MATERIALS:

    cardboard (such as backing from a 5" x 7" paper pad)
    yarn
    scissors
    ruler

HINT: How can you use the yarn to form the vertical threads for your loom? How will you hold them firmly in place?

1. Study the diagram above. Think about how the sets of horizontal and vertical threads work together.
2. Write and sketch your ideas on paper.
3. Now, see whether your loom works. Use thin strips of yarn, or colored paper, in analogous colors as your horizontal threads. Experiment with weaving them on the loom.

Science Objective: The student designs and conducts an appropriate investigation to answer a given question.

Name _____   Date _____

READING A TOPOGRAPHIC MAP

The *Eye Dazzler* is a blanket made by a Navajo. The Navajo have lived in the American Southwest for hundreds of years. Many areas of the Southwest are dry and mountainous. Climate and geography affected the Navajo's culture and way of earning a living.

WHAT TO DO: Use the map and the chart to learn more about Navajo lands. Then, answer the questions.

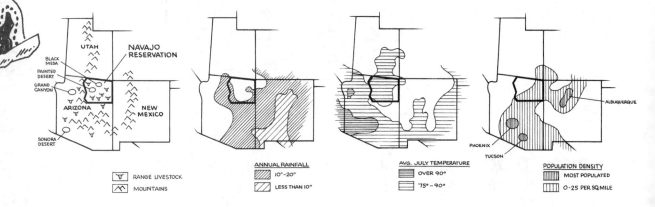

SOCIAL STUDIES

1. What is the average July temperature in northeastern Arizona? _____
2. Circle the words that describe this land.

dry	desert	mountainous	marshy
plains	rainy	farmland	rangeland
urban	rural	wetland	forested
hot	cold	temperate	mesa

3. How many people are there per square mile in this region?_____

4. What work do you think many Navajo do? _____

5. Why do you think weaving is part of the Navajo culture?

_____

_____

Social Studies Objectives: The student uses geographic tools such as maps and atlases to organize, interpret, and share information about people, places, events, and the environment. The student compares and contrasts the ways that various groups during the development of Texas and the United States met their basic needs.

Name _____ Date _____

RHYTHM AND REPETITION

In music, a drumbeat creates a rhythm you can hear. Repeated lines and shapes in the Navajo weaving, *Eye Dazzler*, create a rhythm you can see. What kind of drumbeats does the *Eye Dazzler* suggest to you? There are patterns of thin lines and thick lines. What kinds of sounds might these be? There are lines that zigzag, cross, and turn corners. What patterns of drumbeats might these show?

WHAT TO DO: Compose a drum solo that uses the rhythms and feelings you find in the *Eye Dazzler*. (You might use pencils as drumsticks and a book as a drum.)

1. Describe and practice different drumbeats for these shapes.

 _____

 _____

 _____

 _____

2. Tell how drumbeats for thick lines are different from those for thin lines.

_____

3. Decide how to group drumbeats into phrases. What could diamond-shaped lines represent?

_____

4. "Read" the weaving as a piece of music. Combine the drumbeats as you think they should go. Make your drum solo express the mood of the weaving.

Arts (Music) Objective: The student compares in two or more arts how the characteristic materials of each art can be used to transform similar events, scenes, emotions, or ideas into works of art.

THE ARTS

Name_____ **Date**_____

Artists use analogous hues in artwork to create unity. An analogous color scheme uses hues that are next to each other on the color wheel and share a common hue.

WHAT TO DO: Create a design filled with analogous colors.

1. Select the ◯ shape tool and draw a large circle. Use the ⌑ tool to select half of the circle and delete it. Select the ➘ tool and draw a line to close the semi-circle.

2. Use the ➘ tool and the ▢ and ◯ shape tools to add lines and shapes to the semi-circle to make an interesting design.

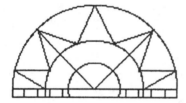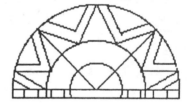

3. Select the design with the ⌑ tool and choose Copy and Paste from the Edit menu to create three duplicates. Use commands from the Selection menu to flip or rotate each copy to make circles or another design.

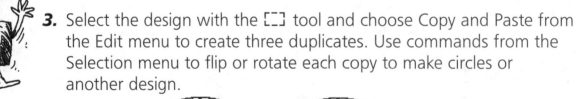

4. Select the ✍ tool and fill the design with color. Use an analogous color scheme for the entire design.

Technology Objective: The student uses software programs with graphics to enhance learning experiences.

48

Name_____ Date_____

SUPPORTING OPINIONS WITH FACTS

When you place complementary colors side by side, the contrast between them appears greater. In the same way, your words can contrast facts and ideas. When people argue two sides of an issue, they bring up contrasting reasons for their opinions. Each side in an argument gives an **opinion,** or belief, supported by reasons and **facts,** which are known to be true.

Issue: **The Intelligence of Dogs**

	FOR	AGAINST
Opinion:	Dogs are the smartest animals.	Dogs are not the smartest animals.
Reasons/ Facts:	They learn tricks.	They do not have the biggest brains.
	They help and protect humans.	They do not have language like dolphins.

WHAT TO DO: Take a side on the following issue. Think of three reasons or facts that support your side.

Issue: Fast food served as school lunches

My Opinion: _____

_____

Reason/Fact: _____

_____

Reason/Fact: _____

_____

State the opinion of someone on the opposite side. Give one fact that contrasts with or opposes your opinion. _____

_____

Language Arts Objectives: The student evaluates uses of propaganda and distinguishes fact and opinion in texts. The student compares and contrasts ideas, themes, and issues within and across texts.

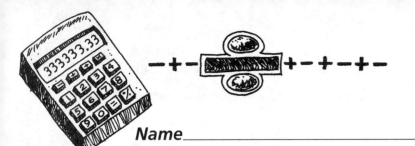

Name_____ Date_____

BUILDING GEOMETRIC SHAPES

Strong colors and shapes make Davis's *Ancestral Spirit Dance* stand out. Find where triangles were used to make squares. What patterns are made with zigzag lines? You can use simple geometric shapes to build more complex, interesting shapes. Many-sided shapes are called **polygons.**

WHAT TO DO: Complete each activity.

1. Decide what simple geometric figures were joined to make these polygons. Use a ruler to draw lines that show the building blocks. List the shapes in each polygon on the lines.

hexagon	parallelogram	trapezoid

_____   _____   _____

_____   _____   _____

2. Now, write the name of each figure described below.

_____ three sides, three angles

_____ four equal sides, four right angles

_____ four sides, four right angles

_____ six sides, six angles

3. On another piece of paper, build a complex polygon with triangles, rectangles, and squares. Write a description of it. Cut it apart like a puzzle. Ask someone to put it together using your description.

Mathematics Objective: The student identifies the critical attributes of geometric shapes or solids.

50

Name _____ Date _____

UNDERSTANDING THE PAST FROM DATA

The featherwork adornment from Peru was found in an archaeological dig. An **archaeologist** studies past times and cultures by digging up and examining things that people left behind. An archaeologist studied the neckpiece closely and collected *data* (information) in order to understand the culture of the people who made and used it. **Artifacts** like the neckpiece give many clues to the past.

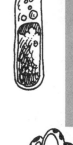

WHAT TO DO: Study the scientist's data. Use it to answer the questions below.

ITEM:	Peruvian neckpiece
AGE:	700 yr.
MATERIALS:	macaw and parrot feathers, cotton backing, cut shell beads
WHERE FOUND:	central coast region, near Lima
CONDITION:	excellent
COMMENTS:	found in burial deposit; images of god and bird figures common in region; feathers from tropical forest several hundred miles inland

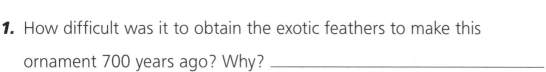

1. How difficult was it to obtain the exotic feathers to make this ornament 700 years ago? Why? _____

_____

2. Did the neckpiece belong to an important person? How do you know? _____

_____

3. What information tells you that farming was part of the culture?

_____

_____

Science Objective: The student uses selected data to reconstruct and interpret past events.

SCIENCE

Name _____ **Date** _____

TEXTILES IN DIFFERENT ERAS

Davis's painting uses an African *textile* (cloth) design. Both it and the neckpiece are things that people could wear. Clothing and adornments change from one era to another. As a society changes, so do its clothing fashions. For example, cloth may change because new fabrics become available or because new methods of producing them may be invented.

WHAT TO DO: Place the development of each type of textile on the time line. Then answer the questions below.

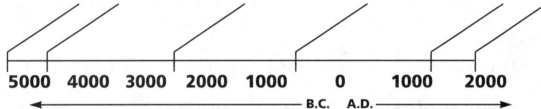

5000	4000	3000	2000	1000	0	1000	2000

B.C.   A.D.

Rayon–thread spun from chemicals from wood and cotton, 1880
Silk–thread spun from the silk of the silkworm, China, 2700 B.C.
Linen–thread made from flax plant, ancient Egypt, (5000 B.C.)
Wool–thread spun from the fleece of sheep, probably before recorded history
Nylon, Polyester–threads spun from plastics, 1940s
Cotton–thread spun from fibers of cotton plant, 500 B.C.

1. Which textiles are made from natural products?

_____

2. Which textiles are human-made products?

_____

3. Which two textiles are oldest?

_____

4. Which textiles require raising animals?

_____

Social Studies Objective: The student gathers information, categorizes it by topic, and organizes it chronologically.

SOCIAL STUDIES

Name _____ Date _____

HOW COSTUME ADDS TO A DANCE

The neckpiece from Peru may have been worn during a *ritual dance*. A ritual dance is a formal, traditional dance that helps celebrate a special occasion or that has a special purpose. Each part of the dancer's costume may also have a meaning or purpose.

WHAT TO DO: Invent a ritual dance for a special occasion. (You may pick one from the list or think of another ritual.) On the lines, describe the costume and any adornments you would wear. Explain how they add to the meaning of the dance.

RITUALS: wedding   birth of a child
              graduation   joining a club

COSTUME:

_____

_____

_____

_____

_____

_____

ADORNMENTS:

_____

_____

_____

Draw pictures of the costume and adornments on the back of this page.

Practice performing your dance. Give a one-minute demonstration for your class. If possible, wear a costume to add to your performance.

Arts (Dance) Objective: The student creates a dance that successfully communicates a topic of personal significance.

THE ARTS

*Name*_____ *Date*_____

Artists use complementary hues, hues that are opposite each other on the color wheel, to create contrast in artwork.

WHAT TO DO: Create a mask filled with complementary colors.

1. Select the ▤ tool or the ✏ tool. Draw a large mask shape.

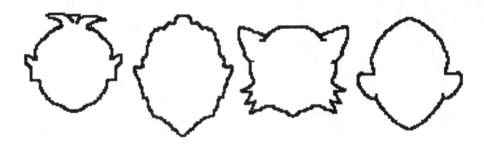

2. Add features to show a certain mood.

3. Use the 🪣 tool to add color to your mask. Choose complementary colors to add to the mood.

Technology Objective: The student uses software programs with graphics to enhance learning experiences.

TECHNOLOGY

Name_____ **Date**_____

USING THE DICTIONARY

Manabu Mabe's painting is titled *Melancholy Metropolis*. What does the title mean? Both words in the title are words you may not know. A **dictionary** can help you learn unfamiliar words. The dictionary gives you pronunciations, meanings, examples, and other information about its **entry words**.

WHAT TO DO: Use a dictionary to help you answer the questions.

1. What does *melancholy* mean?

_____

2. What does *metropolis* mean?

_____

3. What is a *melancholy metropolis?* _____

_____

4. Write the syllables in each word. Mark the syllables that are stressed.

_____

5. Look up the word *warm.* Which meaning for *warm* applies to the artworks in this lesson?

_____

6. List three things you can learn about a word from the dictionary.

_____

_____

_____

Language Arts Objective: The student uses dictionaries to determine unfamiliar words' pronunciations and meanings.

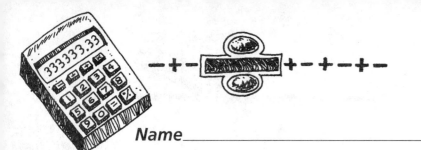

Name_____ Date_____

ESTIMATING

The mask of *Baird Trogon* is made of rows of feathers. It is not important to know the exact number of feathers in the mask. All you need is a reasonable estimate. If there are 17 rows of feathers in each section of the mask and there are 8 sections of the mask, about how many rows of feathers are in the mask?

Because 17 is between 10 and 20, it rounds to 20. Eight rounds to 10.

$20 \times 10 = 200$

There are about 200 rows of feathers in the mask.

WHAT TO DO: Use rounding to solve each problem.

1. Baird Trogon lives on a 30-square-mile island. There are 14 creatures living in each square mile. About how many creatures live on the island? _____

2. The creatures on the island make baskets to sell to visitors. It takes 26 minutes to make a basket. About how many baskets can a creature make in 4 hours? _____

3. The baskets sell for $5.80 each. If the creature sells 11 baskets in a day, about how much money would the creature make?

_____

4. Baird Trogon lives in a tree hut that is 74 feet high. The height of the nearest house is 32 feet. About how much taller is Baird Trogon's tree hut than the house?

_____

Mathematics Objective: The student uses rounding as a tool for estimating reasonable results of problem situations using whole numbers and decimals.

Name_____ Date_____

STARGAZING

The mask of Baird Trogon is made of a pattern of feathers. Patterns exist throughout nature. You can see certain patterns in the stars. People have named **constellations,** or groups of stars, for the shapes they suggest. What does the Big Dipper look like? Because of Earth's movement, familiar stars can be seen at different places in the sky at different times of the year.

WHAT TO DO: Compare the Big Dipper on different dates. Answer the questions about this constellation. Use a ruler to help you measure.

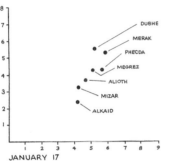
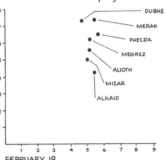

SCIENCE

1. What stars make up the Big Dipper?_____

_____

2. Fill out the table below to show where the stars are on two different dates.

	January 17	**February 19**
Dubhe		
Merak		
Phecda		
Alioth		

3. Look at the grids. Are the stars in the Big Dipper in the same position

on January 17 and February 19? _____

4. How does the Big Dipper change over time? What stays the same?

_____

_____

Science Objective: The student investigates and explains that patterns stay the same even when rotated or seen from different directions.

Name _____   Date _____

MURALS AND MEXICO

Manabu Mabe's painting *Melancholy Metropolis* uses shapes and colors to convey a message about life in a big city. Murals are large artworks painted on the walls of buildings. Many Mexican murals are grand and heroic. Their purpose is to inspire Mexicans' pride in their culture and history. They have also been used to inspire a desire to achieve social goals, such as social equality.

WHAT TO DO: Plan a mural that would represent your community in the past, present, and future. Use the questions as a guide.

- What events and people have been significant?
- What ideals and hopes are important in your community?
- What makes you proud of your community?

Write and sketch your ideas below. Draw a small model of your mural on the back of this sheet. Then, tell what effect you would like your mural to have on people who view it.

_____

_____

_____

_____

_____

_____

Social Studies Objective: The student identifies various ways that language, literature, the arts, architecture, artifacts, traditions, beliefs, values and behaviors contributed to the development and transmission of culture in Texas and the United States.

SOCIAL STUDIES

Name _____ Date _____

USING RESEARCH TO DEVELOP A SCRIPT

Robert Lostutter's artwork shows a creature that is half-person and half-bird. Birds are capable of soaring to great heights. Throughout history, men and women have "soared to great heights" by reaching goals that seemed out of sight. One kind of play, called a **dramatic monologue**, uses only one actor. Through the actor's words, we learn about the person he or she is playing.

WHAT TO DO: Choose a person from the list or a person that you admire. Write a dramatic monologue for the person that will show his or her character.

George Washington	Clara Barton
Sojourner Truth	Sacajawea
Chief Joseph	George W. Carver
Neil Armstrong	Abraham Lincoln
Cesar Chavez	Haing Ngor
Gloria Estefan	Thurgood Marshall
Jane Addams	Albert Einstein
Eleanor Roosevelt	Alexander Bell

1. Choose a historical or present-day person to write about.
2. Do research in books or an encyclopedia to find out about the person.
3. Write your script.
4. At the beginning of the script, describe the setting you would use for your dramatic monologue. Sketch your setting on the back of this page.

THE ARTS

Arts (Theater) Objective: The student applies research from print and nonprint sources to script writing, acting, design, and directing choices.

Name _____ Date _____

Artists use warm or cool colors to create a mood or feeling in their artwork. Artists use hues or colors that have yellow in them to create a warm mood. Artists use hues or colors that have blue in them to create a cool mood.

WHAT TO DO: Create a design filled with warm and cool colors.

1. Select the ☐ shape tool and draw a large square.

2. Use the ☐ and ◯ shape tools to draw smaller shapes inside the large square.

3. Use the ➚ tool to divide the square in half. Use a horizontal, vertical, or diagonal line.

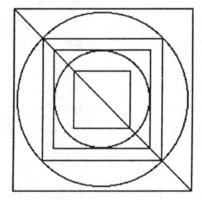

4. Select the ✋ tool and add warm colors to one half of the design and cool colors to the other half.

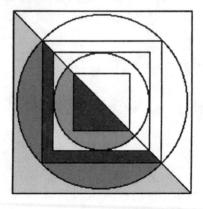

Technology Objective: The student uses software programs with graphics to enhance learning experiences.

60

Name _____ Date _____

HIEROGLYPHICS

Hieroglyphics are an ancient Egyptian form of writing. At first, pictures stood for objects. Later, simpler symbols came to stand for sounds. As *Ipuy and His Wife* shows, Egyptians painted hieroglyphics in their tombs and on monuments.

WHAT TO DO: Study the table to learn which objects represent different sounds. Then, use the information to answer the questions.

i   y   w   b   h   m   s   t   n   r   g   k   l

1. *Ren* was the Egyptian word for *name*. Which hieroglyph says "ren"?

a.

b.

c.

2. Think about what you have learned about hieroglyphics. What can you conclude about the direction in which you read hieroglyphics?

_____

3. Use the chart above to write a hieroglyph for an English word or make up your own hieroglyphs.

Reading/Language Arts Objectives: The student applies knowledge of sound-symbol correspondence, language structure, and text meanings. The student draws conclusions from text information.

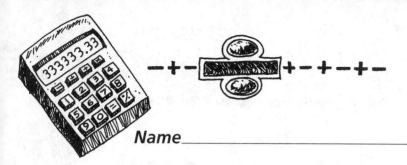

Name_____ Date_____

CALENDARS FOR MEASURING TIME

The ancient Egyptian civilization shown in *Ipuy and His Wife* was advanced. One achievement of this culture was the invention of the calendar. By studying the movements of stars in the sky, Egyptians found that it took about 365 days for certain stars to return to the same place in the sky.

WHAT TO DO: Compare the ancient Egyptian calendar with a current calendar. Answer the questions about measuring time.

Egyptian Calendar

Current Calendar

1997		
JANUARY	**FEBRUARY**	**MARCH**
S M T W T F S	S M T W T F S	S M T W T F S
1 2 3 4	1	1
5 6 7 8 9 10 11	2 3 4 5 6 7 8	2 3 4 5 6 7 8
12 13 14 15 16 17 18	9 10 11 12 13 14 15	9 10 11 12 13 14 15
19 20 21 22 23 24 25	16 17 18 19 20 21 22	16 17 18 19 20 21 22
26 27 28 29 30 31	23 24 25 26 27 28	23/30 24/31 25 26 27 28 29
APRIL	**MAY**	**JUNE**
1 2 3 4 5	1 2 3	1 2 3 4 5 6 7
6 7 8 9 10 11 12	4 5 6 7 8 9 10	8 9 10 11 12 13 14
13 14 15 16 17 18 19	11 12 13 14 15 16 17	15 16 17 18 19 20 21
20 21 22 23 24 25 26	18 19 20 21 22 23 24	22 23 24 25 26 27 28
27 28 29 30	25 26 27 28 29 30 31	29 30
JULY	**AUGUST**	**SEPTEMBER**
1 2 3 4 5	1 2	1 2 3 4 5 6
6 7 8 9 10 11 12	3 4 5 6 7 8 9	7 8 9 10 11 12 13
13 14 15 16 17 18 19	10 11 12 13 14 15 16	14 15 16 17 18 19 20
20 21 22 23 24 25 26	17 18 19 20 21 22 23	21 22 23 24 25 26 27
27 28 29 30 31	24/31 25 26 27 28 29 30	28 29 30
OCTOBER	**NOVEMBER**	**DECEMBER**
1 2 3 4	1	1 2 3 4 5 6
5 6 7 8 9 10 11	2 3 4 5 6 7 8	7 8 9 10 11 12 13
12 13 14 15 16 17 18	9 10 11 12 13 14 15	14 15 16 17 18 19 20
19 20 21 22 23 24 25	16 17 18 19 20 21 22	21 22 23 24 25 26 27
26 27 28 29 30 31	23/30 24 25 26 27 28 29	28 29 30 31

1. How are the two calendars alike?

_____

2. How are they different?

_____

3. On the current calendar, find how many:

_____ weeks are in a year.

_____ days are in a week.

_____ or _____ days are in a year.

Mathematics Objectives: The student uses measurement procedures to solve problems involving time. The student uses ratios to describe relationships between units of measure within the same measurement system.

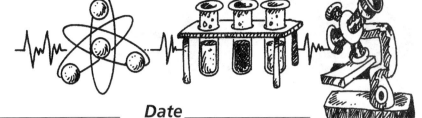

Name _____ Date _____

CHANGES FROM COMBINING MATERIALS

Ipuy and His Wife is a fresco. A fresco is painted on wet plaster. The damp surface absorbs some of the pigment. The picture and the wall combine, and the painting is not *on* the wall but *in* it. When two materials combine, they may make a new material, with new properties (such as a new form, odor, or color). If the combination has new properties, a **chemical change** has occurred. If materials mix but do not take on new properties, a **physical change** has occurred.

> **PHYSICAL CHANGE:** Sand mixed in water
> **CHEMICAL CHANGE:** Baking soda + vinegar

WHAT TO DO: Analyze the experimental paints. Write **chemical** or **physical** in the blank to show what kind of change has occurred.

		RESULT
1.	sand + glue + food color	gritty, sticky semisolid
	_____	
2.	cream + lemon juice + grape juice	purple semisolid
	_____	
3.	butter + chocolate + heat	melted chocolate
	_____	

4. What materials could you combine to make a safe paint for preschoolers? Describe the changes that occur when the paint is mixed.

Ingredients: _____

_____

Result: _____

_____

Science Objective: The student combines two or more materials to create a new material, and compares the properties of the original and the new materials.

SCIENCE

Name _____ Date _____

ADAPTING TO LIFE IN A HOT, DRY LAND

The people in *Ipuy and His Wife* are shown wearing the light, white linen clothes typical in this very hot, dry country. The objects on their heads are perfume cones, which melted in the heat and helped keep them cool. In this desert land, the great Nile River was a lifeline.

WHAT TO DO: Use the information and diagram below to answer the question.

RAINFALL: Almost never, except a little near coast.
POPULATION: 96 percent lived along the Nile River.
NILE RIVER: 4,100 miles long. Flooded every August. Left behind rich black mud from mountains of Ethiopia. Farmers began raising crops in October.

1. Where did most Egyptians live? Why? _____

_____

_____

2. Why was the flooding of the Nile important? _____

_____

_____

3. Egyptians invented a simple machine called a *shaduf* for moving water. Study the diagram and tell how you think the shaduf was used.

_____

_____

Social Studies Objectives: The student identifies how people and physical geographic features affected settlement. The student analyzes and describes how physical geographic features and climate affect everyday life, ways of making a living, and the economy of a region, in both historical and contemporary settings.

SOCIAL STUDIES

Name _____ Date _____

CONTRASTING DANCE MOVEMENTS

Deliverance Disco and *Ipuy and His Wife* are very different artworks. One is totally free in its line, shape, and color; and the other is so controlled that it is rigid. A disco is a dance hall filled with color, light, and sound. The couple moves freely. Ancient Egypt was a strict society. People had less freedom to do as they wished.

WHAT TO DO: Think about the movements of the people in the two artworks. Prepare dance movements to illustrate both paintings.

1. Write adjectives that describe the movements in

   a. *Deliverance Disco:* _____

   _____

   b. *Ipuy and His Wife:* _____

   _____

2. What kind of music would go with the movements from each painting? Describe the music, or name a song.

   a. *Deliverance Disco:* _____

   _____

   b. *Ipuy and His Wife:* _____

   _____

3. Invent hand, body, and foot movements that show these contrasting types of movements. Put them together in ways that suit the music you have chosen. Create a simple dance for Ipuy and another for the disco dancers.

4. Perform your dance. Ask the audience to write down the mood and ideas suggested by your dance.

THE ARTS

Arts (Dance) Objective: Students identify and clearly demonstrate a range of dynamics/movement qualities.

Name_____ Date_____

Artists repeat lines, shapes, and hues to create visual rhythm or movement in artwork. There are five kinds of rhythm: random, regular, alternating, progressive, and flowing.

WHAT TO DO: Create several designs showing different kinds of rhythm.

1. Select from a variety of tools:
Draw a free-form or geometric shape.

Title and save your shape drawing.

2. Select your shape with the ⌐⌐ tool and choose the Copy and Paste commands from the Edit menu to create several duplicates. Arrange the shapes to make random, regular, and alternating rhythms. Choose commands from the Selection menu to flip or rotate a selected-shape.

Title and save each example.

3. Select the 🖌 tool or the ✏ tool and use a varying line thickness. Draw a variety of repeated curved lines to create flowing rhythm.

Technology Objective: The student uses software programs with graphics to enhance learning experiences.

Name _____ Date_____

PREPARING TO RESEARCH

The artists Liotard and van Gogh focus our attention on shoes as an expression of the people who wear them. Types and styles of shoes tell about where people are, who they are, what they value, what kind of lives they lived, and even when they lived. What do you know about shoes? What would you like to know? When you prepare a report, you need to begin by sorting what you need to find out.

WHAT TO DO: Underline one of the topics below, and prepare yourself to research it. Make notes about what you already know about the topic. Then write questions that you want to answer through your research. Use the back of the page if you need more room.

TOPIC I: Changes in Tennis Shoes over the Years
TOPIC II: American Shoes from the Colonists to the Pioneers
TOPIC III: How Shoes Are Made

WHAT I KNOW: _____

_____

_____

_____

_____

WHAT I WANT TO FIND OUT: _____

_____

_____

_____

_____

Reading/Language Arts Objective: The student writes to organize his or her own knowledge about a topic and formulates questions that can direct research.

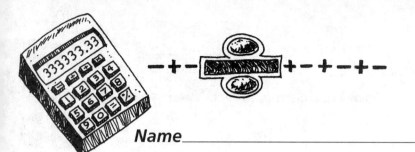

Name_____ Date_____

ESTIMATING

The artworks *A Pair of Boots* and *A Frankish Woman and Her Servant* focus on shoes. People in every age have taken an interest in shoes. However, our society seems especially in love with them. To get shoes that fit well, you must have an exact measurement. It is helpful and practical to understand when you need to get the numbers exactly right and when you can estimate.

WHAT TO DO: For each situation, decide whether you need to measure exactly or you can estimate. Write **exact** or **estimate** in the blank.

1. shoe size to buy new shoes _____

2. length of shoelaces to replace your broken ones _____

3. how much shoe polish to polish your favorite shoes _____

4. how far you walk to and from a friend's house _____

5. how long it takes to dress for school _____

6. size of a button to fit through a buttonhole _____

7. Estimate the lengths of the following articles. Then use a ruler to measure the items and check your estimates.

This page: Estimate _____ Measurement _____

Your math book: Estimate _____ Measurement _____

Your desktop: Estimate _____ Measurement _____

A pencil: Estimate _____ Measurement _____

Mathematics Objectives: The student identifies and describes situations in which an estimate or an exact answer is preferred. The student uses estimation to solve problems.

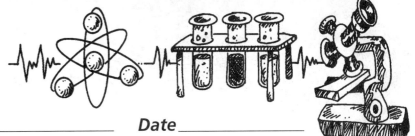

Name _____ Date _____

DESIGNING SHOES

What are the boots van Gogh painted used for? What might be the purpose of the shoes in Liotard's painting?

Can you see any problems you might have because of their design? To **design** something is to plan its form and materials to best fulfill its purpose. Through the ages, different types of shoes have been designed for different purposes. Snowshoes are for walking on the surface of deep snow.

WHAT TO DO: Design a new kind of shoes for walking in water. First, list the characteristics this shoe should have. Second, choose materials for making the shoes. Be sure the materials' properties are suitable for walking in water. Third, sketch your design and label it.

SCIENCE

CHARACTERISTICS OF WATER SHOES

_____

_____

_____

MATERIALS FOR MAKING SHOES

_____

_____

WHAT MY WATER SHOES LOOK LIKE

Science Objective: The student applies his or her knowledge of the properties of matter to solve a design problem.

Name_____ Date_____

LIVES OF PIONEERS

Imagine that the boots in van Gogh's painting belonged to a pioneer in the United States in 1860. The pioneer might have been a **homesteader** in Kansas.

Many homesteaders lived in a sod dugout–the walls, roof, and floor were dirt. Trees were few and far between. Water was precious. The pioneers cleared the tall, tough prairie grass and farmed the flat land. The plow was their most precious possession. If poor weather, insects, or fire destroyed their crop, they might starve.

June 1859–August 1860   No rain; hot winds; water supplies dry up

August 1874   Grasshopper plague; millions eat all vegetation and wood

WHAT TO DO: Use the information about Kansas homesteaders to answer the questions.

1. Why was the plow so important to homesteaders? _____

_____

2. Why were many houses made of sod, or earth? _____

_____

3. In 1860, thousands of pioneers left Kansas. Why? _____

_____

4. About 1874, one Kansas pioneer wrote, "Life was wretchedly uncomfortable, we were poverty stricken." What caused this

situation? _____

_____

_____

Social Studies Objective: The student compares ways various groups during the development of the United States met their basic needs.

SOCIAL STUDIES

Name _____ **Date** _____

WRITING DIALOGUE FOR CONTRASTING CHARACTERS

In Liotard's *A Frankish Woman and Her Servant*, a rich young French woman gestures to her serving girl. What do you think their relationship was like? There can be strong emotion and conflict between people who do not think of themselves as equals.

WHAT TO DO: Decide what each of these characters is like and what they think of one another. Answer the questions about the scene you imagine between them.

1. What is the serving girl carrying? Why? _____

_____

2. What is the woman saying to her servant? What is her tone of voice?

_____

_____

3. What is the girl thinking? How would she show her feelings without

saying a word? _____

_____

4. Write a short dialogue for the two characters. Choose words that show the different concerns and feelings of each one. Write directions about how to say the lines in ( )s.

_____

_____

_____

_____

_____

5. Share your dialogue with a classmate. Model ways each character should stand, move, and talk in the scene.

Arts (Theater) Objective: Students analyze descriptions, dialogue, and actions to discover, articulate, and justify character motivation and invent character behaviors based on the observation of interactions, ethical choices, and emotional responses of people.

THE ARTS

Name_____ Date_____

Artists repeat lines, shapes, and hues to create visual rhythm in artwork. Artists use visual rhythm to express moods.

WHAT TO DO: Create a picture using visual rhythm to express your mood.

1. Select from a variety of tools: 🖌 ＼ ✏ ✒ ▢ ⬭ ◿
   Draw a picture that expresses the mood you are in right now.
   Choose and repeat lines and shapes to create visual rhythm.

2. Use the 🖍 tool to add color to your design. Select colors to match your mood. Choose from a variety of color schemes: monochromatic, analogous, complementary, warm, or cool.

Technology Objective: The student uses software programs with graphics to enhance learning experiences.

TECHNOLOGY

LANGUAGE ARTS

Name _____ Date _____

READING TO LEARN

Artists use different methods to produce their work. The work by Jasper Johns is a *lithograph.* The method of printing lithographs is called *lithography.*

WHAT TO DO: Read to learn more about lithography. Then, use the questions to help you analyze this important printing technique.

Lithography was invented about two hundred years ago. Lithographs were first used to make copies of documents, such as maps and diagrams. (Remember, there were no cameras or copy machines at the time.) Artists soon began to use lithographs for their work.

The word *lithograph* comes from two words meaning "stone" and "write." An artist draws or writes on a flat slab of limestone, using a greasy crayon. The artist then puts acid on the stone. The parts of the stone touched by the acid cause ink to run off, but the crayon marks hold the ink. Then, the artist presses a sheet of paper on the stone. The inked design prints on the paper. Soon after the invention of lithography, printers began to use lighter metal plates. Today, printers use computers and electronic copiers. However, lithography continues to be important in the arts.

1. List three materials lithographers use to make a lithograph.

_____   _____   _____

2. What do printers use today instead of lithography?

_____

_____

3. Why do you think artists still make lithographs, even though printers no longer make copies in that way?

_____

_____

_____

Reading/Language Arts Objective: The student reads to become informed.

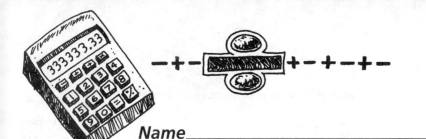

Name_____ Date_____

MEASURING SPACE

Artists use space to create interesting work. The artist knows how positive and negative spaces work together.

WHAT TO DO: Observe and practice ways that mathematicians measure space.

1. Look at the pairs of circles. Shade the space in each pair that you think has the larger area, the inside circle or the remaining space in the outside circle.

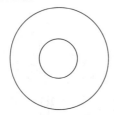
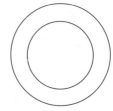

2. Shade the figure with the larger space inside the frame. Then, explain why you chose that figure.

_____

_____

3. Estimate the width of the tarp. Find its area. Will the tarp cover a field with an area of 500 square meters? Explain.

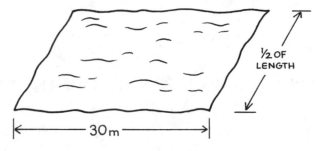

½ OF LENGTH

|←———— 30 m ————→|

_____

_____

Mathematics Objectives: The student explains and records reasoning using objects. The student justifies why an answer is reasonable.

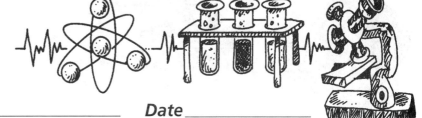

Name _____   Date _____

PATTERNS IN NATURE

Artists use positive and negative space to create new patterns. Where in nature do you find positive and negative space making interesting patterns?

WHAT TO DO: Consider and describe ways that positive and negative space may protect an animal.

1. A hungry lioness watches as a herd of zebras moves by. The lioness sees thousands of stripes: up-and-down stripes and curved stripes—all run together. She can't tell where one zebra ends and another begins. How might stripes save a zebra?

_____

_____

2. The baby giraffe is surrounded by big giraffes. Which one is its mother? Scientists say the baby knows its mother by her skin pattern. Give the giraffe outline a pattern different from its neighbor.

3. This fish lives in shallow creeks that have small pink, tan, and black stones on the bottom. Draw a pattern on the fish that will protect it from predators.

Science Objective: The student interprets and describes behavioral changes resulting from external stimuli.

Name _____ **Date** _____

PABLO PICASSO'S HOMELAND

The artwork by Jasper Johns shows silhouettes of Pablo Picasso. Picasso, one of the greatest artists of the twentieth century, was from Spain. Spain is one of two countries on a large peninsula in Europe. A *peninsula* is a piece of land almost surrounded by water.

WHAT TO DO: With a partner, explore Picasso's homeland.

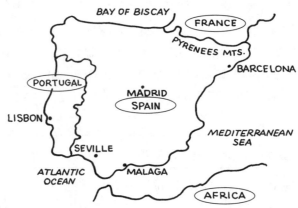

1. What mountains form the boundary between Spain and France?

_____

2. Which other nation shares the peninsula with Spain?

_____

3. Which continent is south of Spain? _____
4. Draw arrows pointing to the cities of Malaga, where Picasso was born, and Barcelona, where he studied.
5. Name three bodies of water that surround Spain.

_____

_____

6. Look at a world map or globe. What other peninsulas do you see? List them.

_____

_____

Social Studies Objective: The student uses maps to organize and share information about a place.

SOCIAL STUDIES

Name _____ *Date* _____

DRAMATIC REVERSALS

Artists use shape reversal to create a work that shows more than one way of looking at an object. A playwright can use reversal, too, to change the way we see or feel about something.

WHAT TO DO: Think of an activity you enjoy, such as a sport or hobby. Imagine a person who does not like that activity. Plan a conversation between you and that person. Use these activities to help you compare ideas and turn your conversation into a one-person play. Write your answers on another sheet of paper.

- List reasons you like the activity you chose.
- List the imaginary character's reasons for not liking it.
- Imagine a conversation with the imaginary person. Would you explain why you enjoy the activity? Would the other person argue with you?

Now turn your conversation into a one-person play. Pretend you are having a conversation with someone about the activity. Walk around, but remember to look at the imaginary person. Use your hands and lots of expression as you explain your reasons for enjoying the activity. Pretend to listen to the other person. Then, argue or explain or persuade. You can be funny or serious. Share your play with the class.

THE ARTS

Arts (Theater) Objective: The student creates characters, environments, and actions to create tension.

Name_____ Date_____

Artists use positive and negative space in an artwork to create interest and sometimes to make visual puzzles. Positive spaces are objects, shapes, and forms in artwork. Negative space is the area around, over, under, and behind the objects, shapes, and forms.

WHAT TO DO: Use positive and negative space to create a shape reversal in an artwork.

1. Select the 🖌 tool and draw the profile of a friend.

2. Use the ⌖ tool or the ⬚ tool to select the profile. Then, choose the Copy and Paste commands from the Edit menu and the flip or rotate command from the Selection menu to create a mirror image.

3. Select the ☐ shape tool to draw a box around the profiles. Add lines to connect the profiles. Title and save the design.

4. Select the 🖌 tool and fill the design with colors to emphasize either the positive or the negative space. You may want to use the ✎ tool for a gradient fill. Create several different combinations. Retitle and save each design.

Technology Objective: The student uses software programs with graphics to enhance learning experiences.

TECHNOLOGY

78

Name _____ Date_____

CREATING ILLUSION IN WRITING

You have seen how an artist uses positive and negative space reversal to create an illusion. When you write a story, you create an illusion as you develop an interesting character.

WHAT TO DO: Show how you would help readers of a story you are writing draw some conclusions about a mysterious or unusual character.

1. Write a sentence describing a mysterious character.

_____

_____

2. Describe one action of the mysterious character.

_____

_____

3. Write a statement in which the character reveals something important about himself or herself.

_____

_____

4. Write a statement in which another character says something about the mysterious person.

_____

_____

5. On another sheet of paper, write a short story using the character you developed.

Reading/Language Arts Objective: The student writes to inform, using description and narration.

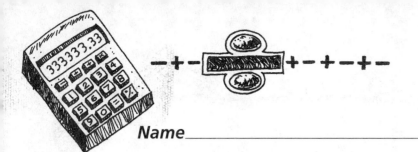

Name_____ Date_____

LOOKING FOR PATTERNS

M. C. Escher creates a pattern of shapes in *Sky and Water.* Items in any pattern are related to one another in an important way and are arranged in some order.

WHAT TO DO: Describe the mathematical pattern in each section below.

1. Describe the pattern in this row of fractions and write the next

two fractions in the pattern._____

_____

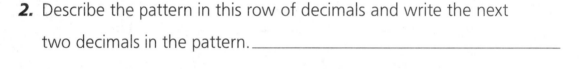

1/2   1/4   1/8   1/16   _____   _____

2. Describe the pattern in this row of decimals and write the next

two decimals in the pattern._____

_____

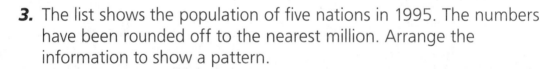

.1   .4   .7   1.0   _____   _____

3. The list shows the population of five nations in 1995. The numbers have been rounded off to the nearest million. Arrange the information to show a pattern.

Canada	29 million
Japan	125 million
Mexico	92 million
Nicaragua	4 million
United States	261 million

Mathematics Objective: The student finds patterns and makes generalizations from charts and tables.

Name _____   Date _____

REPTILES IN DANGER

Real-life reptiles are as fascinating as Escher's lizard. Many reptiles throughout the world are endangered or threatened.

WHAT TO DO: Discover some facts about sea turtles, one of the many kinds of reptiles. Analyze each set of facts. For each set of facts, write a sentence telling what else you need to know to understand why the sea turtles are endangered.

1. Female sea turtles come ashore to dig pits in the sand of beaches, where they lay hundreds of eggs. Baby turtles scratch their way to the surface and head toward the ocean. Most do not reach water.

_____

_____

2. Poachers visit the beaches at night to steal eggs to sell for food.

_____

_____

3. Many poachers are poor people who need the money they make from selling the turtle eggs.

_____

_____

4. Each year there are fewer beaches where sea turtles can safely lay their eggs.

_____

_____

5. Fishers using nets often trap turtles by mistake.

_____

_____

Science Objective: The student analyzes data to determine if further investigation is necessary.

Name_____ Date_____

A COUNTRY CLAIMED FROM THE SEA

M. C. Escher lived in the Netherlands. This country is an excellent example of how people can change their environment.

WHAT TO DO: Use the information below to describe how the Dutch manage to live in their low country.

- About half of the Netherlands is below sea level at high tide, which occurs every day.
- In the 1100s and 1200s, the people built dikes to keep out the sea. A dike is a kind of wall around the land.
- Long ago, wind-powered pumps drained the land. Today, diesel and electric pumps are used.
- The Dutch dug canals, which are waterways that are similar to rivers.
- The canals, pumps, and dikes keep Holland drained.

In your own words, explain the following statement. Use the facts listed above. *If it were not for the hard work of its people, half of the Netherlands would flood every day.*

_____

_____

_____

_____

_____

_____

Can you think of another example in which people have changed their environment? Describe it. Tell whether the change was good or bad.

_____

_____

_____

_____

Social Studies Objective: The student shows how people have adapted to and modified their environment.

Social Studies (sidebar)

Name _____ **Date** _____

ANIMAL MOVES

An artist uses space to create an illusion. Dancers can also use space to create illusions.

WHAT TO DO: Think about how a reptile, bird, or fish moves. Experiment to create the illusion of an animal's movement. These activities will help you create a dance.

1. With your fingers, show how lizards move. If you aren't sure, ask a classmate to help you. List four words that describe how lizards move.

_____

_____

2. Use one hand to imitate a bird in flight or a bird on the ground. With a partner, experiment with movements that create the illusion of a bird.

3. Use your body to imitate the movements of a fish.

4. On a sheet of paper, draw a floor plan to show how you plan to move in the space you have chosen.

5. What sounds go with the movement of the animal you have selected? Can you make these sounds with your feet? With your hands? Try different methods.

_____

_____

_____

6. With a partner or group, or on your own, move through a space. Add the sound of wind, water, or scratchy sand around your animal. When you are ready, share your dance with the class.

THE ARTS

Arts (Dance) Objective: The student transfers a spatial pattern from the visual to the kinesthetic.

Name_____ Date_____

Tessellations are a type of shape reversal that changes quickly and fits together like a puzzle.

WHAT TO DO: Create a tessellation design.
1. Select the ☐ shape tool and draw a rectangle.

2. Select the ✏ tool or the ✒ tool and draw a design on one side of the rectangle.

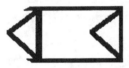

3. Use the 🔲 tool to select the part of the rectangle with the design on it. Choose Copy and then, Paste from the Edit menu and drag a new copy to the other side of the rectangle.

4. Use the ▱ tool to erase extra lines.

5. Select the shape with the 🔲 tool and choose Copy and Paste from the Edit menu. Drag a new copy of the shape next to the original shape so the two shapes fit together like a puzzle. Continue to fit new copies of the shape together by choosing Paste from the Edit menu and dragging the selected shape to a new location.

Technology Objective: The student uses software programs with graphics to enhance learning experiences.

TECHNOLOGY

Name_____ **Date**_____

EXPRESSING THOUGHTS THROUGH WRITING

In art, texture creates an illusion and a mood. When you write, you might also want to create an illusion and share a mood.

WHAT TO DO: Imagine that you are taking tickets as people come in to visit John Pocketts's caravan. Imagine the visitors in the list below. Write a short dialogue that tells what each pair is thinking and feeling about the caravan.

1. two boys about twelve years old

_____

_____

_____

2. two girls about twelve years old

_____

_____

_____

3. an elderly man with his grandson

_____

_____

_____

4. an elderly woman with a large, furry, friendly dog

_____

_____

_____

Reading/Language Arts Objective: The student produces engaging writing through dialogue.

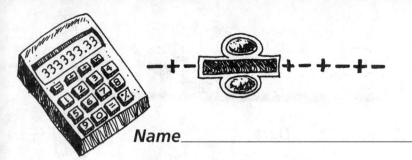

Name_____ Date_____

MATH

DECORATIVE MATH

Artists and carpenters use mathematical principles to create designs such as those on John Pocketts's caravan.

WHAT TO DO: Create a caravan for the year 2010. Use three-dimensional figures to form a wide stripe along the side of your caravan.

1. Brainstorm ideas for creating an interesting and unusual design. Think of many different geometric shapes, such as cubes, cones, or spheres.

_____   _____

_____   _____

2. Choose two or three forms from your list. Draw each one in as many positions as possible: sideways, flipped, upside down, and at different angles.

3. Create a pattern that you like with the forms you have chosen. Think about colors and textures. When you are ready, draw your design on the side of the van below.

Mathematics Objective: The student uses reflections and rotations to make geometric patterns.

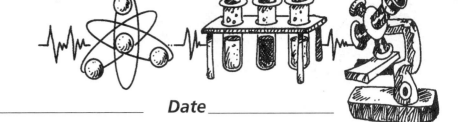

Name_____ Date_____

A CLEANER SOURCE OF ENERGY

John Pocketts's caravan did not pollute the air with an engine. If you built a caravan, how could you reduce its pollution?

WHAT TO DO: Use these facts to help you decide how you can use passive solar energy for some of your needs.

Solar power can heat water. You will need:
• a collector tilted toward the sun (This collector must be large enough to hold the amount of hot water you need in a day–about 70 liters.);
• a small pump for water circulation;
• a tank to store heated water for later use.

Solar energy can heat a room. You will need:
• large windows facing the sun;
• a ceiling fan.

With a partner, use your skills in estimating measurements and needs.
1. Discuss the height, width, and length of a van.
2. Estimate the size of water collectors (you know the size of a one-liter bottle), storage tanks, and windows.
3. Decide how the needs of a moving home will differ from those of a house. Can you use passive solar power in a caravan? Explain why or why not.
4. What would be the benefits of using this energy source? What would be the drawbacks?
5. Summarize your findings in a paragraph. On the back of this page, make a sketch showing your van after you have added the solar equipment.

_____

_____

_____

_____

Science Objective: The student understands the use of the sun's energy to cause change.

Name _____   **Date** _____

TEXTURE IN TEXTILES

A photograph helps you imagine textures. The clothes you are wearing are examples of textures you can feel.

WHAT TO DO: Evaluate ways inventions and discoveries have changed the way people dress.

Early humans probably wore animal skins. But soon they discovered that animal hair and some plants and seeds could be twisted together to make yarn, and the yarn could be woven to make cloth.

Over 7,000 years ago, flax was woven into linen cloth, and 4,000 years ago, men and women wove wool into cloth. It was just 200 years ago that machinery was invented to spin and weave with great speed. A machine could make cloth that always looked the same and that had a tighter weave. In the last fifty years, synthetic fabrics have become common; nylon and orlon, for example, are made from chemicals and plastics, not animal fur or plant fibers.

Materials made by weaving fibers are called *textiles*. The word *textiles* comes from the Latin word *texere*, which means "to weave." Another English word from *texere* is *texture*. So you see, your clothes get their texture from being textiles.

With a partner, do these activities on another sheet of paper.
1. Draw a time line showing the history of textiles.
2. Examine five pieces of clothing. List the materials. Describe the texture of each. Tell how texture makes the material comfortable or uncomfortable to wear.

Social Studies Objective: The student evaluates the impact of inventions on the lives of Americans.

SOCIAL STUDIES

*Name*_____ *Date*_____

TEXTURE IN A BALLAD

The textures in John Pocketts's *Caravan* give the piece visual interest.
Music has texture, too. The texture of music comes from weaving
words, rhythm, and melody together to make a whole.

A *ballad* is a song that tells a story. Each verse in a ballad has four
lines. The second and the fourth lines rhyme. Lines are often repeated,
and the words are simple. Rhyming and repeating lines give ballads
their texture.

WHAT TO DO: In a ballad, tell a story about a caravan. Analyze
what you think about when you look at the photographs of *Caravan.*
Imagine that you have a caravan. Where will you go in your caravan?

1. Think of a story that takes place as you travel in your caravan.
2. Write a verse of your ballad. Express a mood: Is it carefree, scary, or
   lonesome?

_____

_____

_____

3. Write a second verse that has a different mood.

_____

_____

_____

4. Think about how the two moods fit in one song.
5. Write words and music for your song. With a small group, plan to
   perform it. You can sing it alone or with a group, with or without an
   instrumental accompaniment. You may choose to record your song
   and play it later.

_____

_____

_____

Arts (Music) Objective: The student composes a short piece within a specified guideline, demonstrating how
the elements of music are used to achieve unity and variety, tension and release, and balance.

THE ARTS

Name_____ Date_____

Artists use visual texture to create interest and emphasize an area in artwork.

WHAT TO DO: Draw a room inside your home with visual texture.

1. Draw a room in your home. Include many kinds of objects and details.

Select from a variety of tools:

2. Add visual texture to some of the items so it looks like you could touch them.

Use the ⬩ tool or the ✐ tool to draw lines and shapes.

Use the ◁ tool with a selection from the pattern choices.

Technology Objective: The student uses software programs with graphics to enhance learning experiences.

90

TECHNOLOGY

Name_____ Date_____

LANGUAGE ARTS

FORM SHAPES COMMUNICATION

For artists, a *form* is an object that has length, width, and depth.
For a writer, *form* is the way he or she chooses to present ideas.

WHAT TO DO: Write to share an experience. The experience may be
real or imaginary. The following steps will help you get started with your
writing.

1. Name the experience. Example: "the time I slept in a cave"

_____

_____

2. Decide what your purpose is in sharing the experience. Do you
want to entertain, persuade, explain, teach, or describe a mood?

_____

3. What form will help you with your purpose? Think about writing a
poem, a story, or an essay. A journal can make your experience seem
real. Choose a form.

_____

4. State your main idea.

_____

_____

5. On a separate sheet of paper, write your first draft. Exchange
drafts with a partner and share ideas. Write a final draft.

Reading/Language Arts Objective: The student chooses the appropriate form for his or her purpose for
writing.

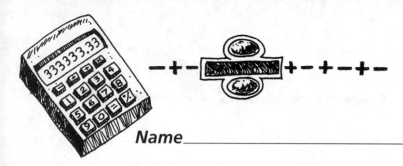

Name_____ Date_____

FARAWAY PLANETS

Space stations as large and as advanced as the one in Robert McCall's painting have yet to be built. Much of the information we have about our solar system was gathered by unpiloted space probes like *Voyager 1* and *Voyager 2*.

WHAT TO DO: Compare the explorations of the *Voyager* space probes by answering the questions below.

These *Voyager* probes did not land on the planets but came near enough to get information.

Voyager 1 was launched in September 1977. In March 1979, it was within 170,000 miles of Jupiter. By November 1980, the craft was 78,000 miles from Saturn.

Voyager 2 was launched in August 1977. It arrived at a spot 400,000 miles from Jupiter in July 1979 and was 63,000 miles from Saturn in August 1981. *Voyager 2* went on to Uranus and Neptune. It was 3,100 miles from Neptune in August 1989. Both probes are now in interstellar space (space outside the solar system).

1. Which probe took longer to arrive near Jupiter? How much longer, stated in months, did it take?

_____

_____

2. Which probe came nearer Jupiter? How many miles nearer?

_____

_____

3. Which came nearer Saturn? How many miles nearer?

_____

_____

4. How many months did it take *Voyager 2* to arrive 3,100 miles from

Neptune? _____

Mathematics Objective: The student uses addition and subtraction strategies to solve problems involving whole numbers and decimals.

Name _____ Date _____

EXERCISE FOR HEALTH

Roger Brown's space station looks like an earthly neighborhood. If a space station were more like your home, do you think you would get homesick? Would you be healthier?

WHAT TO DO: Examine the following facts about the ways people stay healthy. With a small group, discuss the questions below and write your answers on a separate sheet of paper.

When you exercise, you use your body to make it healthier. Lifting an object shortens some of your muscles. Lowering the object lengthens them. Both activities increase your blood circulation and breathing rate. Regular exercise also makes bones stronger, increases your strength, and helps you control weight.

When your great-grandparents were young, few people exercised for fun. The work they did was exercise. Nearly everyone scrubbed floors, hung clothes on a clothesline, cut the grass with a scythe or a push-mower, walked behind a plow, or climbed in and out of trucks and wagons to deliver heavy packages. Of course, many people still do these things, but their work is made easier by machines, and many people get almost no exercise from their work. To keep healthy, people today must choose recreation that includes exercise.

1. Name three things you do that cause your muscles to shorten and lengthen.
2. What kind of work can you do at home or at school that is like work done in your grandparents' time?
3. How have attitudes about exercise changed since your grandparents were your age?
4. Design an exercise program that uses movements from different kinds of work. For example, lifting hand weights from the floor to above your head imitates the motions of hanging clothes on a line. Describe at least three exercises.

Science Objective: The student predicts outcomes after gathering and measuring data that show change.

Name _____ Date _____

TOPOGRAPHICAL MAPS

Artists use shading to create the illusion of form. Mapmakers can also create the illusion of form on a flat surface. A map that shows the landforms in an area is called a *topographical map*.

WHAT TO DO: Interpret the map below and answer the questions. Then on a separate sheet of paper, make a map of your city, state, or neighborhood. Use a key and shading to show landforms.

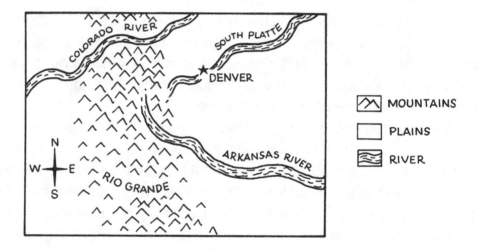

SOCIAL STUDIES

1. Which part of Colorado has the most tall mountains?

_____

2. Which part of the state is lowest?

_____

3. On which river is the capital of Colorado?

_____

4. Explain how the map helps you understand Colorado's landforms.

_____

_____

_____

Social Studies Objective: The student uses and creates geographic tools, such as maps.

Name _____ **Date** _____

MUSIC OF SPACE

Form has a place in music as well as in other kinds of art. Think about the way words, rhythm, and melody fit together in your favorite song. That pattern, or form, separates it from other kinds of music.

WHAT TO DO: Read the paragraph below. Work with a small group to create your own musical form.

Many hundreds of years ago, no one yet dreamed of a solar system, outer space, or space stations. But people looked up and gazed at millions of beautiful stars. They wondered how everything they saw fit together. Some folks of that early time thought that the universe was made up of spheres inside of other spheres. All of these spheres moved around one another at different speeds, and as they moved, they made wonderful music.

Pretend that the old idea of the music of the spheres is true. What do you think the music would sound like? What objects would you need to imitate the music? Do you need something that creaks, squeaks, hums, buzzes, or whistles? Will regular instruments help? Electronic instruments? Voices?

Form a group of composers. Discuss all of the questions above. Then, plan a musical composition that will be fun to listen to. Try to make it sound like the music of the spheres surrounding Earth.

THE ARTS

Arts (Music) Objective: The student uses a variety of traditional and nontraditional sound sources and electronic media when composing and arranging.

Name_____ Date_____

Artists add textures to shapes to create the illusion of three-dimensional forms in artwork.

WHAT TO DO: Use a variety of textures to show the forms of an outer space home or station.

1. Begin to draw your view of space architecture. Use many kinds of shapes.

Select from a variety of tools:

2. Create the illusion of form by adding lines and shapes and by using different shading techniques.

3. Add a background. Overlap shapes.

4. Add more textures with the tool and a pattern selection.

Technology Objective: The student uses software programs with graphics to enhance learning experiences.

96

TECHNOLOGY

Name _____ Date _____

BUILDING UNDERSTANDING

Architects can use drawings, photographs, and words to describe a building. A writer often needs to use both words and pictures to share an idea with readers.

The mysterious cottage in the forest had only one room. One wall was made of gold. It had a big picture window overlooking a garden filled with flowers of red, yellow, and purple. One wall was a huge mirror. One wall held shelves containing hundreds of books. The fourth wall was covered with video screens. On each screen the figures of a different video game danced. Strange beeps and whirs from the many games made a noisy chorus in the cottage.

WHAT TO DO: You can probably imagine the room described. But you could not expect a first-grade reader to understand all of the words. For first-graders, you would probably draw a picture to go with the story to help them understand.

Write a three-page story for a beginning reader. Describe a mysterious place. Use easy words. Then, work with a partner to plan illustrations for the story. When you have a story and drawings that really work together, make a final copy and bind the pages together to make a book for a first-grade reader. Use the space below for brainstorming.

_____

_____

_____

_____

_____

Reading/Language Arts Objective: The student produces communications using appropriate media.

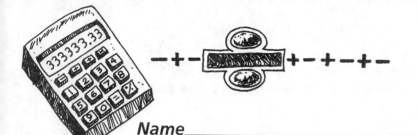

Name_____ Date_____

USING MATH TO BUILD

Frank Lloyd Wright and Elizabeth Plater-Zyberk created buildings for special spaces, using tools from the science of mathematics.

WHAT TO DO: Plan a home to fit the environment shown in the diagram. Answer the questions to help you with your planning.

1. Which side of the space gives the best view? Which rooms

should be on that side? _____

_____

2. Which side will be quietest? Which rooms should be on that side?

_____

3. What will be the total area covered by your house? _____

4. What is the area of the yard around the house?_____

5. What material will make the house blend into its surroundings?

_____

6. Which architectural forms will you use in the house?

_____

- On a separate sheet of paper, draw a large diagram of the lot shown below. Cut out paper strips to form room boundaries. Move them around on the diagram as you plan the rooms for your house. When you decide on a plan, make a final diagram, showing the area of each room.
- Sketch the outside of your house. Use shading and color to show architectural forms and the materials you chose to build the home.

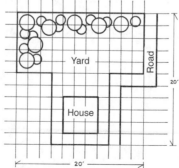

Mathematics Objective: The student selects tools, such as real objects or manipulatives.

Name _____   Date _____

INVESTIGATE TO SOLVE A PROBLEM

Architects plan buildings that fit into their surroundings. They need information from scientists about an area's natural resources to help them decide whether buildings should or should not be built.

WHAT TO DO: Analyze the following information about a small town. Should the town be encouraged to grow?

Water Station is a very small town—about a hundred twenty families live there. It's a pretty place. People have green lawns that they water every day. They grow beautiful flowers, too. Water Station is very hot in the summer. Houses and buildings are air-conditioned. A park in town is cool because of a huge fountain at its center. Two years ago the town built an Olympic-sized swimming pool.

Water Station is in a very dry part of the United States. Only ten or twelve inches of rain fall in an entire year. There is no underground water here, so people can't dig wells. Instead, they use water from a canal dug between two very large rivers. These rivers also supply water to several very large cities, and farmers use the water to irrigate large farms. Some people in Water Station want to see the town grow. They would like to see more businesses. They want better incomes. So, they are talking about building 30 or 40 more homes at the edge of town.

You have been asked to help with the planning. What must you know to make a good decision? On another sheet of paper, write at least five questions you want answered before you say yes or no to the people who want a larger town.

Science Objective: The student designs and conducts an appropriate investigation to answer a question.

Name ______________________ **Date** __________

HOMES THAT FIT

Frank Lloyd Wright designed structures that would blend in with the environment. Homes must often be built to suit their environment.

WHAT TO DO: Make your own design for a home that blends in with its environment.

Over five hundred years ago a Spanish explorer named Coronado led his soldiers northward. They came to a camp near the present-day border between Texas and New Mexico. The buildings in the camp were cone-shaped tents wrapped in buffalo hides. Coronado described the dwellings as "tall and beautiful."

A tent home used by other native peoples was dome-shaped. These buildings were made from poles that could be bent to form a dome. Bark from trees, or mats woven from reeds and branches, were used as cover.

In other parts of the continent, Native Americans built permanent homes. Pueblos were made of sun-dried clay bricks. In other places, homes were built of logs or planks. In each place, the house fit into its surroundings, used available materials, and helped the people live safely and comfortably.

1. Why do you think Native Americans in some parts of North America made their homes of buffalo hides while those in other areas made homes of sun-dried clay bricks?

____

____

2. Look at a map of the United States. Choose an area where you might like to live. Describe the natural resources and landscape of the area.

____

____

3. On a separate sheet of paper, sketch your home design.

Social Studies Objective: The student analyzes and describes how physical geographic features and climate affect everyday life.

Name _____ Date _____

MOVING TOGETHER TO BUILD A DANCE

Many very simple buildings are built quickly by people who are willing and able to work together. Dancers must also work together to present a dance.

WHAT TO DO: Have you ever watched a barn raising or seen one on television? Imagine a frame like the one below. The sides of the barn are lying on the ground. Decide what workers must do to pull up the sides of the barn. Work with a small group of barn raisers. In a dance, interpret a barn raising.

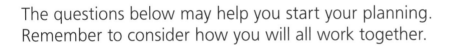

The questions below may help you start your planning.
Remember to consider how you will all work together.

- How will you move your hands? _____

- Your arms? _____

- Your bodies? _____

- What will you do first? _____

- Next? _____

- Finally? _____

- How can you celebrate when the barn is finished?

_____

- Perform your barn-raising dance.

Arts (Dance) Objective: The student demonstrates the ability to work cooperatively in a small group during the choreographic process.

Name_____ Date_____

Architects use a combination of geometric forms to design buildings and spaces for living, working, and leisure.

WHAT TO DO: Draw a house or apartment building using architectural shapes.

1. Select from a variety of tools: ◁ ◯ ☐ ⟍
Draw the building using geometric shapes.

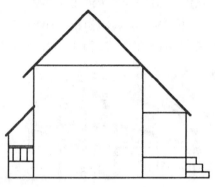

2. Add lines to create depth.

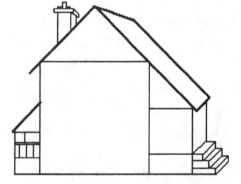

3. Add the geometric shapes found in doors and windows.

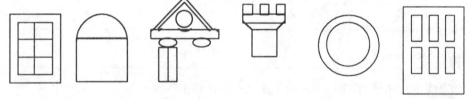

4. Add details, textures, and shading. Select from a variety of tools:

Technology Objective: The student uses software programs with graphics to enhance learning experiences.

TECHNOLOGY

Name _____ Date _____

MAKE YOURSELF CLEAR

Decisions about public buildings are usually made by committees. They review many ideas, but in the end, they must agree on one.

WHAT TO DO: To convince others of a good idea, you must elaborate on that idea by giving clear reasons to support it. To judge someone else's ideas, listen carefully to supporting reasons.

A cafeteria has been built for your school. One long wall has no doors or windows. The architect wants your class to plan something to put on that wall. You have one class period to agree on a plan.

1. Work alone to come up with at least two plans.
2. Come together in groups of three to five. Share ideas. Select one or two of the best ideas. Be sure you can support the ideas you are suggesting. The two ideas are:

_____

_____

Choose a spokesperson to share the ideas with the class.
3. Hold a class discussion of ideas. Remember, consider only the ideas supported by reasons. Make a decision.
4. Which idea did you personally like best? _____

_____

Why? _____

_____

5. Write your class decision here.

_____

_____

6. What were the most convincing reasons?

_____

_____

Reading/Language Arts Objectives: The student listens to interpret messages by understanding the major ideas and supporting evidence. The student uses appropriate vocabulary to describe ideas, feelings, and experiences clearly.

Name_____ Date_____

DATA THAT DESCRIBE AUSTRALIA

The Sydney Opera House is one of the best-known sights of Australia. There is much more to learn about this beautiful continent known as "the land down under."

WHAT TO DO: Use mathematics to help you describe and compare the area and populations of the different parts of Australia.

State	Population	Area (sq. km)
New South Wales	5,800,000	801,000
Queensland	3,000,000	1,800,000
South Australia	1,400,000	984,000
Victoria	4,400,000	228,000
Tasmania	458,000	68,000
Western Australia	1,700,000	2,500,000

1. Australia has six states and two territories. The total population of Australia is 18,000,000. About 290,000 people live in the Capital Territory, and 170,000 live in the Northern Territory. How many live in the six states?

_____

2. The table shows the populations of six states. What is the range of populations? What is the median population?

Median _____

Range _____

3. Use the chart to find the range and median of the areas of the six Australian states.

Median _____

Range _____

4. Give the population per square kilometer of each state.

_____

_____

_____

Mathematics Objective: The student uses mode, median, and range to describe and compare sets of data.

Name _____   Date _____

CHANGES OCCUR OVER TIME

Le Corbusier was born in Switzerland among the towering Alps. His church, Notre Dame du Haut, was built in the mountains of France.

WHAT TO DO: Investigate the mountains that Le Corbusier knew. Understand the sequence of events that formed these mountains.

The Alps are Europe's newest mountain range. They have not yet been worn down to low, rounded stumps by wind and water. They are still tall and steep.

The Alps were formed by folding. Earth is made up of plates that are always moving. They move very slowly, but with great force. When two plates move together, they push upward and long ranges of mountains can form. This happened in the region of the Alps perhaps 50 million years ago. They are limestone mountains, indicating that a sea once covered this part of the world.

About two million years ago, huge glaciers filled the valleys in the Alps. As the glaciers moved, they dragged along tons of gravel and rock. When the glaciers melted about 10,000 years ago, these piles of rock, called *moraines,* remained. Often the moraines dammed up rivers and created cold mountain lakes. The Alps have deep valleys as well as high mountain peaks. Mont Blanc (4,807 meters) is the highest peak in the Alps.

1. On the another sheet of paper, create a time line that shows how the Alps were formed, starting 50 million years ago.
2. How do you think the Alps will change in another million years? Write a prediction. Use evidence from the article to support your prediction.

_____

_____

Science Objective: The student compares and contrasts events in which changes have occurred over time.

Name _____   Date _____

USING EVERYDAY KNOWLEDGE TO SOLVE PROBLEMS

Architects often use forms from nature as a basis for their designs. Think about natural forms in your area such as mountains or bodies of water.

WHAT TO DO: Consider whether natural forms in your region could be used as the basis for the design of a public building. Work with a small group to plan the building.

1. What natural forms are found in your area? Are there prairies like those that inspired Frank Lloyd Wright? Is there sand, a mountain, or a large lake? List natural forms that you know of in your area.

_____   _____

_____   _____

2. Think about a building that already exists near the place where you will construct your public building. Describe the forms and

shapes of that building. _____

_____

3. Examine the three architectural forms below. Draw a fourth form of your own. Then, select one form for your new building. Explain why

you chose it. _____

_____

Social Studies Objective: The student applies problem-solving and decision-making skills to resolve contemporary problems.

SOCIAL STUDIES

Level 5, Unit 3, Lesson 6
ART CONNECTIONS:
Form and Tactile Texture

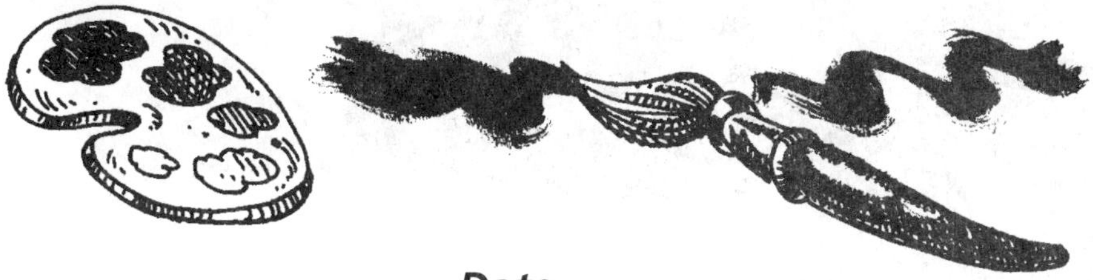

Name ______________________ ***Date*** ____________

WHAT DOES IT FEEL LIKE?

In a play, only the actor can actually experience tactile texture. Sometimes, an actor must find ways to share this experience of touch with the audience.

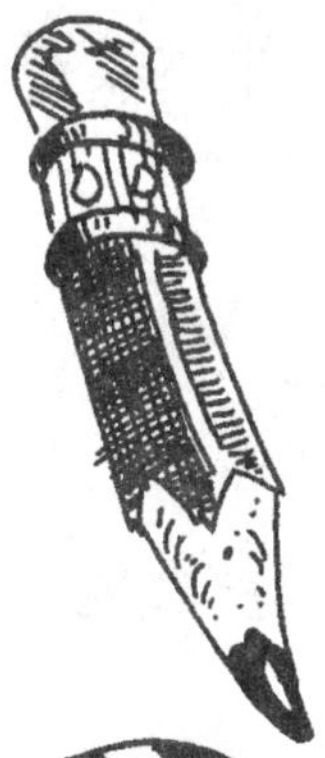

WHAT TO DO: With a small group, experiment with ways a character might share a tactile experience with an audience. Use the activities below. Write stage directions to help an actor express the texture he or she is feeling.

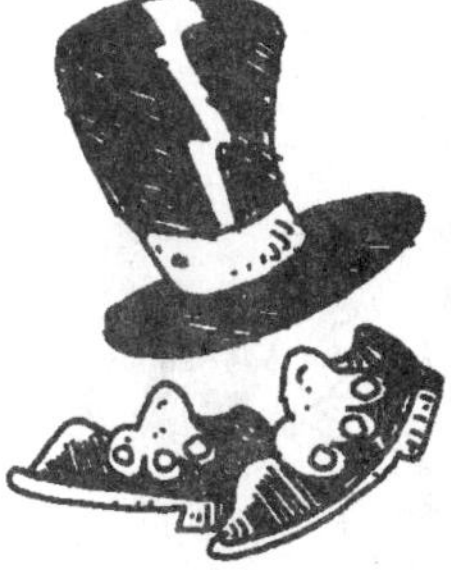

1. Mercy is incredibly hot as she runs in the race. Then, she runs through the cold, wet spray of a hose.

2. It is pitch dark. Kwok feels his way through the alley, moving his hand along the jagged edge of a fence.

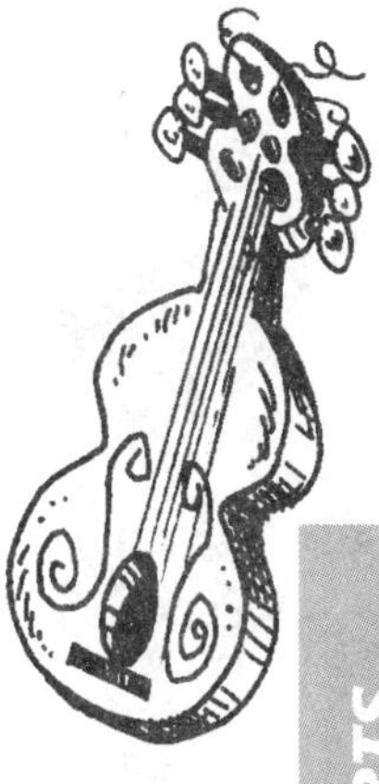

3. Ben walks barefoot on the hot beach.

4. Marcella loves her new dress, but the tag in back scratches her neck.

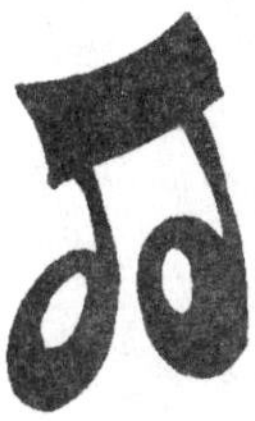

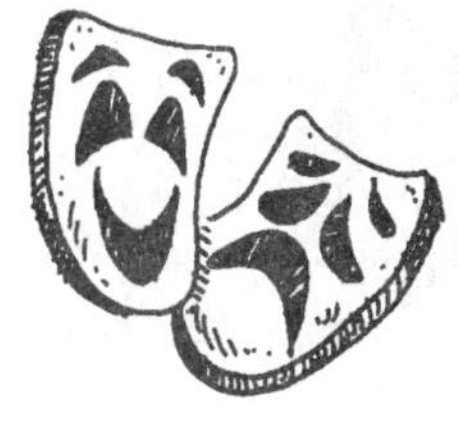

Arts (Theater) Objective: The student leads groups in planning visual and aural elements in improvised and scripted scenes, demonstrating group and consensus skills.

Name_____   Date_____

Architects design structures for public purposes. Sometimes the designs are based on shapes found in nature. Architects consider building materials and the setting.

WHAT TO DO: Design a public building for your local community.

1. Select from a variety of shape tools: 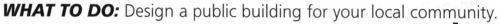 and the 🖌 tool or the ✏ tool. Draw a public building by combining geometric and free-form shapes. Consider the setting, building materials, and objects in nature for ideas.

2. Add lines and shapes to show depth and form.

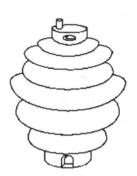 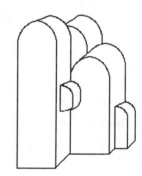

3. Add shading or patterns to give the structure more depth and form. Use a variety of tools: 🖌 ✏ ◻ 🪣

4. Add details and objects to show the setting.

TECHNOLOGY

Technology Objective: The student uses software programs with graphics to enhance learning experiences.

108

Name_____ **Date**_____

KEEPING THINGS IN PROPORTION

In art, proportion shows how large or small an object is in relation to another part. In your life, a sense of proportion shows how important a person, object, idea, or act is in relation to another.

WHAT TO DO: Examine the following old tales. Explain how someone in each story saw something, or failed to see it, *in proportion to* other events or ideas.

1. "In Jack and the Beanstalk," Jack was pleased to get some magic beans in trade for the cow. Why was his mother not pleased? What did each of them think was important?

   _____

   _____

2. A mouse, caught by a lion, promised to help the lion if he would let her go. The lion laughed, but let her go. Later, the mouse chewed through a net and freed the lion. What did the mouse think was important?

   _____

   _____

3. A princess who got everything she ever asked for cried because she didn't have the moon. Give a real-life example of someone like the princess.

   _____

   _____

4. Winter was coming. While the grasshopper played, the ant collected food. What did each character think was most important? Which one was wiser?

   _____

   _____

Reading/Language Arts Objectives: The student draws inferences and supports them with text evidence and experience; The student uses writing as a tool for reflection and exploration.

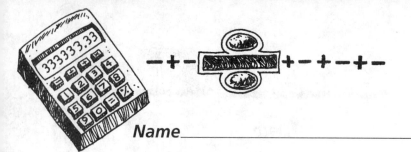

Name_____ Date_____

IN PROPORTION

Artists use proportion, the relationship in size of one part to another. Proportions can be expressed in several ways. Ratios can help you find proportions.

WHAT TO DO: Discover more about proportion as you analyze each problem below.

1. Which of the following expressions shows the relationship of an object 2 centimeters long to an object 4 centimeters long?
a. 2 x 2 = 4   **b.** 2:4   **c.** 2/4   **d.** 2 x 4 = 8

_____

2. State the relationship of rectangle A to rectangle B as a fraction.

_____

A [   ]

B [   ]

3. The average adult is about 7 1/2 heads tall. A young child is about 5 1/2 heads tall. A baby is about 3 heads long.
a. What is the height in meters of a man whose head measures 30 cm from chin to crown?

_____

b. About how long is a baby whose head is 15 cm long?

_____

c. Kim is fourteen years old. What number do you think expresses the proportion of her head to her total height? Explain your answer.

_____

_____

Mathematics Objective: The student uses ratio to describe relationships between units of measure within the same measurement system.

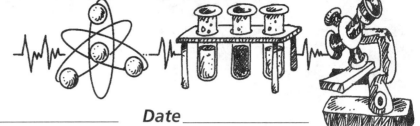

Name _____ Date _____

SEEING IN COLOR

Goya is known for his skill in using light and color to create portraits of wealthy persons.

WHAT TO DO: Learn more about color by planning your own investigation.

People who are color-blind cannot see some or all colors. For most people, light reflecting from an object onto their retina causes them to see color. Light is a form of energy that behaves like waves. Light waves come in different lengths, or *wavelengths.* We see different colors when objects *absorb* or *reflect* different wavelengths of light energy. For example, pigments in paints absorb and reflect different wavelengths of light. The red paint on a stop sign absorbs light waves with short and medium wavelengths, like violet, blue, and green. It reflects longer light waves from the red end of the color spectrum, which makes the stop sign appear red.

We also see color when light is *refracted,* or bent. When light passes through a glass prism, the different wavelengths bend at different angles, which separates the light into bands of color. Raindrops can act as tiny prisms, separating sunlight into the bands of colors that we see in a rainbow.

Design an investigation to answer one of the questions. On another sheet of paper, make a list of all the questions you will need to answer and the materials you will use in your investigation.

1. In what order do refracted colors appear?
2. What gives pigments their color? For example, what makes red paint red?
3. If white light shines through a blue filter, how will each color change?

Science Objective: The student designs and conducts an appropriate investigation to answer a given question.

Name_____ Date_____

FIRST STEPS TOWARD DEMOCRACY

In the eighteenth century, European artists, such as Goya and Robert often painted portraits of wealthy and noble people. Later in the century, some European countries changed forever as poorer people fought to gain power in government. At the same time, life was changing in America, too.

WHAT TO DO: Explore changes in America and France in the eighteenth century. On a separate sheet of paper, draw a time line to show the period from 1774 to 1795. List several of the following events on the time line. Then, answer the questions.

1774   American colonists condemn their unfair treatment by the British government.
1775   The American Revolution begins.
1778   France helps the Americans fight against England.
1783   The Revolutionary War is over.
1789   In France, angry people condemn unfair treatment by their government. They riot and free prisoners in the Bastille.
1789   A new government is formed in France.
1792   Louis XVI, King of France, is put into prison.
1793   France is declared a republic in which the people can choose their leaders.
1793   The king and queen of France are executed.
1793   French people blame the nobles for their problems. Many noble families are executed.
1795   France adopts a new constitution.

1. How were the changes in America and in France alike?

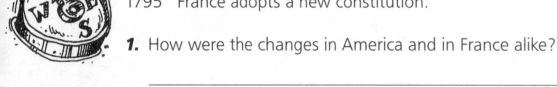

_____

_____

2. How were the changes in America and France different?

_____

_____

Social Studies Objective: The student examines ways individuals can be involved in participatory government.

Name _____ Date _____

EXPRESSING THOUGHTS IN A MONOLOGUE

Posing for an artist such as Hubert Robert would take a great deal of time and patience. Imagine yourself to be one of the people shown in Robert's drawing. What thoughts go through your head as you pose?

WHAT TO DO: Talk about the thoughts you have as you pose in a *monologue,* a speech in which only one person talks. You can just think "out loud" to yourself or you can talk to your audience. Use the chart to brainstorm ideas for your monologue.

Character you will portray:	
Feelings you want to share:	
Facial expressions and movements that express those feelings:	
Words and phrases to share your feelings and ideas:	

When you have finished brainstorming, talk about your planned monologue with a partner. Then, write your monologue or make an outline to follow when you act it out. Practice the monologue with your partner. Then, share your monologue with the class.

THE ARTS

Arts (Theater) Objective: The student demonstrates acting skills to develop characterization.

Name _____ Date _____

Artists use proportion to show the size relationship of one part to another.

WHAT TO DO: Create a proportional drawing of a classmate or teacher.

1. Select the tool with a small brush, the ✏ tool, or the ⬭ shape tool. Draw the head of a classmate or teacher.

2. Use a pencil and the sighting technique to estimate the number of heads tall your model is. Create a guide reflecting that number in order to finish your drawing with the right proportions.

   Use the ✐ tool to select the head you drew. Then, choose Copy and Paste from the Edit menu and paste down the screen the correct number of copies for your guide.

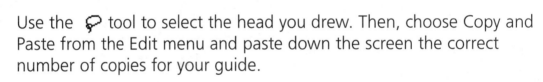

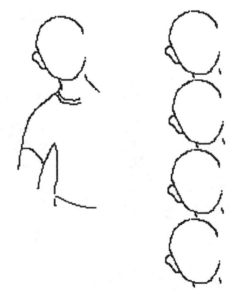

3. Complete the drawing in proportion. Continue to use the sighting technique for body proportions. Then, erase your guide with the ✐ tool.

Technology Objective: The student uses software programs with graphics to enhance learning experiences.

114

TECHNOLOGY

LANGUAGE ARTS

Name_____ Date_____

WRITE A CONVERSATION

The artists have each chosen to show a father and son together. Study both portraits carefully. Consider why these fathers and sons are together.

WHAT TO DO: Explore the relationship between the father and son in one of the portraits. Write a short story about them. Include a conversation between the two people. The following activities will help you organize your story.

1. Write the name each character will use to address the other.
2. Write a dialogue that sounds natural. However, remember that these people lived more than 300 and 500 years ago, respectively!
3. Write a draft of your story. Read it and make any needed changes.
4. Write a revised copy. Take care to use correct punctuation, especially for the dialogue.
5. Exchange stories with a partner. Suggest corrections and improvements for each other's story.
6. Publish the final version of your story for classmates.

Notes for a first draft: _____

_____

_____

_____

_____

_____

_____

_____

_____

Reading/Language Arts Objective: The student selects and uses voice and style appropriate to audience and purpose.

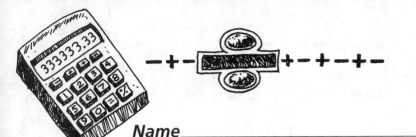

Name_____ Date_____

GEOMETRIC FORMS IN ARCHITECTURE

Domenico Ghirlandaio often painted architectural forms in the background of a portrait. Do you see geometric forms in the architecture painted in the portrait of Francesco Sasetti?

WHAT TO DO: Learn more about geometric forms by using them in these activities.

1. List the geometric shapes you see in the background of Ghirlandaio's painting.

_____   _____

_____   _____

_____   _____

2. On drawing paper, sketch a *skyline,* the outline that city buildings make against the sky. Use three regular polyhedrons, spheres, and parts of spheres. Label each form.

Regular polyhedrons
A *tetrahedron* is a pyramid with four equilateral triangles as faces.
A *cube* has six squares as faces.
A regular *octahedron* has eight equilateral triangles as faces.

Mathematics Objective: The student uses critical attributes to define geometric shapes and solids.

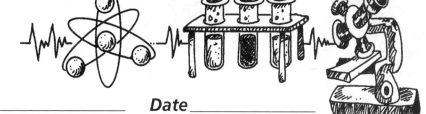

Name _____   Date _____

THE HIMALAYAN ECOSYSTEM

North of Agra, the city in which Emperor Shah Jahan and his son lived, is a range of mountains called the Himalayas. This is the tallest mountain range in the world.

WHAT TO DO: Explore ways life can survive in one part of the Himalayas. The mountain range contains several different climates.

On the slopes of the highest mountains (more than 4,900 meters above sea level), snow cover is permanent. Of course, not many plants grow above this snow line.

Between 4,900 and 3,700 meters, where the temperature rarely rises above freezing, the slopes are covered with small shrubs, grass, and moss.

Below 3,700 meters, there are trees. Most of the animals of the Himalayas live below the tree line.

Select one of the climates described above. What kinds of animals could live there? Use the chart to brainstorm facts and conclusions. On the back of this paper, describe and draw a make-believe animal that could live in the ecosystem you selected.

Climate Facts   **Animal Qualities**

_____   _____

_____   _____

_____   _____

_____   _____

Science Objective: The student creates a make-believe organism that has characteristics and structures appropriate for life in a given ecosystem.

SCIENCE

Name _____   Date _____

GRAPHING MOUNTAIN HEIGHTS

Scale deals with size relationships. It refers to size as measured against a standard reference. In measuring mountains, feet or meters are the standard reference. The tallest mountains in the world are in the Himalaya mountains. However, it is very difficult to measure a mountain exactly, and great arguments have taken place about whether Mount Everest or K2 is the tallest mountain. Most scientists agree that Everest is taller if the same system of measurement is used for both mountains.

WHAT TO DO: Create a bar graph to show the relative heights of the world's ten tallest mountains and the tallest mountain in North America. Use the information on the chart below, but round off the numbers to the nearest hundred.

Mountain Name	Height in meters
Everest	8,848
K2	8,611
Kanchenjunga	8,598
Lhotse	8,501
Makalu	8,470
Dhaulagiri I	8,172
Manaslu	8,156
Cho Oyu	8,153
Nanga Parbat	8,126
Annapurna I	8,078
McKinley (Alaska)	6,194

1. Choose a scale for your graph. For example, one space on the grid could represent 1,000 meters or 500 meters.
2. Write mountain heights (using your scale) on the vertical axis.
3. Write the mountains' names on the horizontal axis.
4. Draw a sketch that represents the mountains on the graph.

Social Studies Objective: The student creates a graph.

SOCIAL STUDIES

Name _____ **Date** _____

USING SCALE TO MAKE A POINT

An artist may use unrealistic scale to emphasize the difference between two figures. You can also use unrealistic scale in a theater production to emphasize a contrast.

WHAT TO DO: Plan a play for a very young audience. Use unrealistic scale to show that a scary character is really not very powerful.

1. Join a group of four or five students to plan a play with at least three characters. One of these should be a scary creature. In the play, tell about some children who meet the creature but find a way to make it powerless. Use a story you have read or heard, or make up your own story. Design a costume for your scary creature. It should make your monster look larger than the other characters. Describe the costume.

_____

_____

_____

2. It is important that the audience understands that in the end the creature has no power. How can your costume change to make the creature look smaller than other characters?

_____

_____

_____

_____

_____

_____

_____

_____

THE ARTS

Arts (Theater) Objective: The student creates characters and environments that create tension and suspense.

Name _____ Date _____

Scale refers to the size relationship of an object compared to a standard reference. Scale can be realistic or unrealistic.

WHAT TO DO: Draw a scene that shows an unrealistic scale.

1. Select from a variety of tools: 🖌 ✏ 🗋 ╲ ▭ ⬭ ⌐
Draw an indoor or outdoor scene. Draw objects the size you would expect to find proportionate to each other.

2. Add one object that is not to scale.

Technology Objective: The student uses software programs with graphics to enhance learning experiences.

TECHNOLOGY

Name_____ **Date**_____

WRITE A LETTER TO AN ARTIST

Every artist approaches a subject in a different way. Renoir and
Raphael used light, color, and expression differently.

WHAT TO DO: Study the two portraits in this lesson. Select the artist
whom you would most like to have paint your portrait. Write him a
letter, inviting him to come to America and create a new painting. In
your letter, discuss the artist's living arrangements, his work space, and
the payment you are offering.

Remember that your letter is a business letter. Use the proper form
for such letters. Use the space on this page for your draft. Write
your final letter on stationery.

_____

_____

_____

_____

_____

_____

_____

_____

_____

_____

_____

_____

Reading/Language Arts Objective: The student produces cohesive written forms.

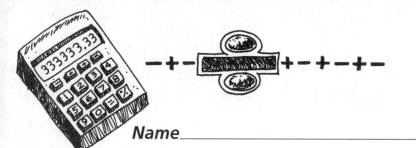

Name_____ Date_____

SYMMETRY

Artists use guidelines to make portraits that are realistic. Drawing a vertical line through the center of a sketch of a face helps an artist make the two sides of a person's face balanced. An object is symmetrical if a line can be drawn through its center, resulting in identical shapes on both sides. In math, we can use lines to find figures that are *symmetrical,* or balanced.

WHAT TO DO: Explore symmetry in mathematics as you complete each section below.

1. Draw the line or lines of symmetry through each figure that is symmetrical. Note that some figures may have more than one line of symmetry.

 A 　　B 　　C 　　D

2. Show the line of symmetry on each drawing.

3. In a realistic portrait, would an artist draw a face that was perfectly symmetrical? Why or why not?

_____

_____

_____

4. With a mirror, look carefully at your own face. Is it perfectly symmetrical?

_____

_____

Mathematics Objective: The student identifies patterns created by reflections and rotations.

Name _____ **Date** _____

GET A SENSE OF YOUR WORLD

A person's face is much more than something to look at. The face is the part of the body through which one takes in a great deal of information about one's surroundings.

WHAT TO DO: Discover more about the sense organs located in the head, and examine the work they do. Name the sense organ identified by the adjective in the list below. Use a dictionary if you need help.

1. olfactory _____   **4.** tactile _____

2. visual _____   **5.** auditory _____

3. flavor _____

Work with a partner. Find one object listed under each sense. Sense each object with only the sense that is listed. Answer the questions to record your responses to your sensory experiences.

6. Which experiences helped you sense an object in a new way?

_____

7. Which objects would be better experienced using a different sense?

_____

8. Which of the objects can be sensed best by using just one sense?

_____

9. Which of the objects can be best sensed by using several senses? Describe why using each sense is important.

_____

_____

SCIENCE

Sight	Touch	Sound	Taste	Smell
apple	tree	tree	paper	apple
glass of water	flower	water running	cloth	blade of grass
ice cube	pencil			

Science Objective: The student assesses accuracy of data collected from biological and physical investigations.

Name _____ Date _____

PIONEERS IN THE WOMEN'S MOVEMENT

Margot Bérard was a little girl at a time when few women became well-known for their work. Women did not have the same rights as men. A movement was beginning to make it possible for women to vote and to do many different kinds of work.

WHAT TO DO: Research each woman listed below. Explain the change each one is responsible for.

Florence Nightingale (1820-1910)

_____

_____

Berthe Morisot (1841-1895)

_____

_____

Mary Wollstonecraft (1759-1797)

_____

_____

Nellie Bly (1867-1922)

_____

_____

Susan B. Anthony (1820-1906)

_____

_____

Which of the changes brought about by these women do you think was most important? Explain why.

_____

_____

_____

Social Studies Objective: The student compares and contrasts how people have adapted to and modified their environments.

SOCIAL STUDIES

Name _____ **Date** _____

MATCHING MOOD TO MUSIC

Both Raphael and Renoir painted interesting faces. Study the portraits and the expressions shown by the subjects.

WHAT TO DO: Respond in music to the mood shown by Altoviti's or Bérard's expression.

1. Name a mood or feeling you see in each face.

Altoviti: _____

Bérard: _____

2. Select one painting for your response. Write a statement about the expression of the face in the painting.

_____

_____

3. Select a type of music that fits the subject's appearance and mood. Describe the music you have in mind.

_____

_____

_____

4. Write a four-line song or instrumental composition to accompany the picture. If you wish, sing or play it for a small group or for the class.

_____

_____

_____

_____

_____

_____

Arts (Music) Objective: The student compares how characteristic materials of two arts can transform similar emotions into works of art.

THE ARTS

Name _____ Date _____

Artists use proportion to help them correctly organize the features of a face in their artwork.

WHAT TO DO: Draw a front view and side view of your head in proportion.

1. Select the 🖌 tool, the ✏ tool, or the ⬭ shape tool. Draw a head shape on the left side of the screen.

2. Use the ➚ tool to draw three horizontal guidelines.

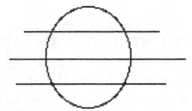

3. Using the lines as a guide, add proportionate features.
   A. Add eyes half way down the head shape.
   B. Draw the nose midway between the eyes and the chin.
   C. Add the mouth between the nose and chin.
   D. Include other features such as your ears, eyebrows, and hair.

4. Draw the profile view of your head next to the front view. Look at the front view as a guide. Compare proportions.

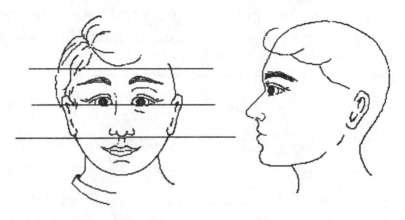

Technology Objective: The student uses software programs with graphics to enhance learning experience.

TECHNOLOGY

126

Name _____ Date _____

SYNONYMS IN DESCRIPTIONS

Portrait painters such as Botero and Modigliani must know the materials of their art well in order to describe a person. Writers and readers must know their materials well, too. Words with similar meanings, called *synonyms,* are useful when writers are describing. Although the meanings of synonyms are similar, they are also slightly different and tell something different about the thing being described.

WHAT TO DO: Think about how using different synonyms helps a writer interpret an idea. Then, learn some words that will help you understand art and artists.

1. Did you think of the word *large* when you saw *Ruben's Wife?* Look at these synonyms for *large.* Use a dictionary or thesaurus to learn the differences. Use the words in sentences.

| rotund | inflated | puffed up |
| grand | monumental | |

_____

_____

_____

_____

2. Look up these words, which are often used in articles about art and artists. Use each word in a sentence.

retrospective   show   fresco   self-taught

_____

_____

_____

_____

Reading/Language Arts Objective: The student uses dictionaries, glossaries, and other sources to determine unfamiliar words' pronunciations and meanings.

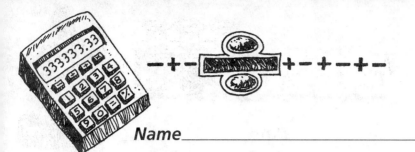

Name_____ Date_____

COMPARING PRICES

Artists may exaggerate to create mood. Mathematicians, however, depend on accuracy.

WHAT TO DO: Explore the advantage of having accurate information when dealing with numbers.

1. Eladio and Consuelo Juarez and their three children, who are between the ages of 9 and 13, are interested in a special exhibit of Botero's paintings at The Gallery. Study the ticket prices below. Describe at least three choices of tickets that the family has. Compare total costs; then explain which choice you believe they should make and why it is the best choice.

Admission to The Gallery	students	$ 2.00
	adults	$7.50
Tickets to the special exhibit	students	$ 3.50
	adults	$12.50
Regular Family Membership (Regular Family Membership does not include admission to special exhibits.)		$45.00
Special Family Membership per year (Special Membership includes free admission to all special exhibits.)		$70.00

_____

_____

_____

_____

2. Which choice of tickets would be best for your family? Explain why.

_____

_____

Mathematics Objective: The student describes everyday situations using mathematical language and symbols.

MATH

Name _____   Date _____

ROCKS AND MINERALS AS ART MATERIALS

Look at the interesting colors in the portrait by Modigliani. The materials that give paints their colors are called pigments. Some pigments come from rocks or minerals. Sculptors also use many different kinds of rocks and minerals in their media.

WHAT TO DO: Evaluate the minerals and rocks listed below. Each has a common use.

Mineral/Rock	Properties
chalk	skeletons of tiny sea animals; soft; usually whitish in color
clay	very fine grains; feels sticky when wet; hardens when dry
graphite	one of the softest minerals; loosely held together
marble	variety of textures and colors; hard and long-lasting; easily cut and polished
talc	the softest of all minerals; easily ground

1. Which mineral or rock is most unlike the others listed? Explain.

_____

_____

2. Which of the minerals and rocks would be useful to artists?

_____

_____

3. Which mineral has a household use? _____

4. Find out how one of the rocks or minerals changes with heat, cold, pressure, or friction. How might an artist take advantage of this change? _____

_____

Science Objective: The student predicts outcomes after gathering and measuring data that show change.

SCIENCE

Name _____   **Date** _____

MAP OF COLOMBIA

Fernando Botero grew up in Colombia in northern South America. Art has been an important part of Colombia's history. Hundreds of years ago, Indian artists sculpted huge stone statues and crafted beautiful gold jewelry. During the 1900s, Colombia has produced a number of internationally known artists and writers.

WHAT TO DO: On the map, label the three regions of Colombia, the country's two largest cities, the mountain range, and the surrounding countries and bodies of water. Use symbols and a key to show features such as mountains and the capital city.

The Andes Mountains divide Colombia into three major regions— the highlands, the coastal lowlands, and the eastern plains. The climates in these regions are different, with the hottest climate being in the lowlands along the coast.

Colombia has a very long coastline, which is divided by the isthmus of Panama. Colombia's west coast is on the Pacific Ocean; the northern coast is on the Caribbean Sea.

South of Colombia, on the Pacific, is Ecuador. Peru, which lies just east of Ecuador, also borders Colombia to the south. Colombia shares its eastern boundaries with Venezuela and Brazil.

Colombia's capital city, Bogotá, is high in the Andes, more than 2,590 meters above sea level. Bogotá is an important center of education, literature, and art. Medellín, the second largest city, lies in a mountain valley about 240 kilometers northwest of Bogotá.

SOCIAL STUDIES

Colombia————

Social Studies Objective: The student creates graphic tools such as maps.

Level 5, Unit 4, Lesson 4
ART CONNECTIONS:
Ruben's Wife and
Portrait of a Polish Woman

Name _____ **Date** _____

EXAGGERATED MOVEMENTS

The artists Modigliani and Botero exaggerated human characteristics to create art. Performing artists also use exaggeration. They can use exaggerated movements to communicate attitudes or moods.

WHAT TO DO: Interpret a mood by using exaggerated body movement in a dance. With a partner, do the brainstorming activity below to get started. Then, plan a dance that a large group can do together. Make it fun.

- Choose a mood everyone can experience. _____
- Experiment with hand gestures, body movement, and steps that show the mood you selected. Describe your movements.

_____

_____

_____

_____

_____

- Now exaggerate the movements you practiced.
- Choose six or eight movements that work best. By using these movements in a pattern, create a dance with steps that are easy to learn and remember. Describe the music's title.

_____

_____

_____

_____

- Choose music that fits the mood.
- Go through your dance several times until you are sure it works.
- Teach your dance to the class. Let everybody enjoy it.

THE ARTS

Arts (Dance) Objective: The student demonstrates accurate memorization and reproduction of movement sequences.

Name _____ Date _____

Artists sometimes exaggerate features to express ideas and feelings in their artwork.

WHAT TO DO: Create a cartoon character using exaggeration to show a mood or expression.

1. Select the 🖌 tool with a small brush, the ✏ tool, or the ◯ shape tool. Draw a head shape for a cartoon character. Consider using the Brush Mirrors command from the Options menu, if available.

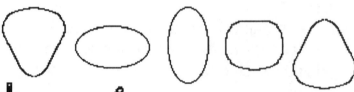

2. Use the 🖌 tool or the ✏ tool to draw features to match the shape and the mood you would like to express. Use exaggeration for some features.

3. Add a body.

Technology Objective: The student uses software programs with graphics to enhance learning experiences.

TECHNOLOGY

Name _____ Date _____

LISTENING FOR DISTORTION

Artists may use distortion to emphasize an idea. Distortion changes a feature. Ideas and words can be distorted also. What happens when someone twists an idea?

WHAT TO DO: Evaluate the need for accuracy in an informative speech. Find ways to avoid distortion in a speech. Learn to recognize it in speeches given by others.

Distort is from a Latin word that means "to twist." Here are three ways writers and speakers can "twist" facts. The examples are from a speech by a student who wants the school to send runners to a marathon 100 miles away.

Sarcasm: words or examples chosen to make fun of someone or something
> Example: *The school won't take money from our wonderful football team to pay for ordinary, boring runners like me.*

Generalization: statements using words such as always, everybody, mostly, most, every time, they
> Example: *Everybody knows they always help the football team.*

Unsupported statements: stating facts without evidence
> Example: *Sending us to the marathon won't cost as much as sending a football team to the next game.*

1. State your position on a plan not everyone agrees with. You might suggest that your school, family, or neighborhood take some action.
2. Write a two minute speech explaining your plan. Avoid all forms of distortion.
3. Present your speech to a small group. Listen to speeches by other students. Evaluate each speech. Discuss any use of distortion.

Reading/Language Arts Objectives: The student evaluates a message in terms of its content, delivery, usefulness, and credibility.

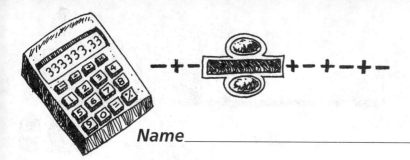

Name_____ Date_____

TOPOLOGY

Makers of masks achieve distortion by bending, warping, stretching, squashing, or twisting materials. In mathematics, *topology* is the study of how bending, stretching, shrinking, and twisting affect the properties of geometric figures.

WHAT TO DO: Experiment with topology. Use a material that can be stretched and twisted without breaking. Topologists often use a sheet of soft rubber, but paper will do if you are careful not to tear it. Do the topology activities. On another sheet of paper, take notes on what you discover. Share and evaluate your discoveries with a group.

1. Make a Möbius strip. Here's how: Cut a long, thin, rectangular piece of paper. Twist it once; then glue or tape the ends together. Next, draw a line around the whole strip. What did you notice about the ends of the line you drew?
2. Make another Möbius strip. This time, poke a hole anywhere in the center of the strip and begin to cut. Cut along the center of the strip until your scissors reach the place where they began. What did you notice about the Möbius strip after you cut it?
3. With a piece of string, or a shoe lace, tie a simple overhand knot. Count the number of points where one lace crosses another. If you are left-handed, ask a partner who is right-handed to tie an overhand knot for you. Compare the two knots.
4. A *torus* is the shape of such common objects as doughnuts, hoops, rings, and tires. Describe a torus without using any examples.

Mathematics Objective: The student explains and records reasoning using objects, words, pictures, symbols, and/or technology.

Name _____ *Date* _____

ANIMALS AND THEIR ENVIRONMENTS

Masks are often used in ceremonies celebrating people's relationship with nature. Many scientists today are expressing concern for natural environments.

WHAT TO DO: Learn more about the environment of New Zealand.

About 84 percent of the animals native to New Zealand are found nowhere else in the world. Scientists believe that New Zealand's animals developed without any contact with animals from other islands and continents for over 100 million years.

Before the Maoris brought other animals with them to New Zealand, the only animals on the islands were birds, lizards, frogs, and two species of bats. One of these animals is the tuatara. The tuatara is the only reptile that has survived from the age of the dinosaurs.

Many kinds of flightless birds were also native to New Zealand. The kiwi and takatre still live in the forests. Some other birds, including a huge bird called a moa, were hunted until they became extinct. Many of them were killed by people. Others were destroyed by dogs and rats that came with the humans. Settlers also brought deer, goats, rabbits, and opossums to New Zealand.

Discuss questions of survival with a partner and report your conclusions.
1. How do you think animals respond if a predator appears where

there have never been predators before? _____

_____

2. Why were moas and other flightless birds easy to hunt?

_____

_____

3. How could nonpredators like deer change an environment and

destroy it for native animals? _____

_____

Science Objective: The student examines interactions between the organisms within an ecosystem that support the organisms' survival.

SCIENCE

Name_____   Date_____

HOW ONE CULTURE HAS ADAPTED TO CHANGE

Tlingit masks are part of the artistic tradition of an old culture that has had to adapt to many changes in its environment.

WHAT TO DO: Answer the questions to compare two ways of life.

1. The Tlingits have lived in the area we now call Alaska for thousands of years. Their homes, boats, and artworks were made from the wood available in abundant forests. In 1741, invaders arrived in Alaska from Russia. In 1867, the United States purchased Alaska from Russia. These outsiders cut down the forests and later built pipelines to carry oil from the north. How do you think these changes affected the lives of the Tlingits?

_____

_____

_____

2. Tlingits went to sea in huge wooden dugouts. The Tlingits relied on fish, sea mammals, and mollusks to feed and clothe their families. Oil pipelines and the growth of large cities polluted the ocean. How do you think this change affected the lives of the Tlingits?

_____

_____

_____

3. If you were a Tlingit, how would you deal with the changes brought by outsiders? Which parts of your traditional culture would you work to keep?

_____

_____

4. Which parts of the modern world might make your life better?

_____

_____

Social Studies Objective: The student compares and contrasts ways people have adapted to an environment.

SOCIAL STUDIES

136

Name _____ Date _____

EFFECTS OF DISTORTED SOUND

Artists use distortion when working with clay, metal, and paint. Musicians sometimes use distorted sound to express or emphasize moods and ideas.

WHAT TO DO: Choose a song or piece of instrumental music that expresses a mood. Change the mood by distorting musical sounds.

1. Experiment with ways to distort your voice.
   a. You make sounds by using lungs, vocal cords, tongue, teeth, lips, and nose. List at least five ways you can distort a note

   by manipulating these organs. _____

   _____

   _____

   b. What can you add to a voiced sound to distort it? List some

   methods that work well. _____

   _____

   _____

2. Experiment with ways to distort sound from an instrument.
   a. What can musicians use to distort sounds from horns?

   _____

   _____

   b. What distorts the sound of a piano? An organ?

   _____

   _____

   c. How would you distort the sound of a stringed instrument?

   _____

3. With a partner, select an effect you want your music to have. Use your voice or an instrument. Then, experiment with distortion until you have the effect you want. Practice and perform the piece of music you chose.

Arts (Music) Objective: The student uses a variety of traditional and nontraditional sound sources and electronic media when composing and arranging.

THE ARTS

Name_____ Date_____

Distortion is altering a feature so that it does not look normal.

WHAT TO DO: Create an expressive mask with distorted features to express a mood or idea.

1. Select the 🖌 tool with a small brush, the ✏ tool, or the ⬭ shape tool. Draw a mask shape. Consider using the Brush Mirrors command from the Options menu, if available.

2. Add distorted features that express a mood or idea.

3. Add lines, shading, and visual textures. Choose hues and patterns to help express the mood. Select from a variety of tools: 🖌 ✏ 🗋 🖌

Technology Objective: The student uses software programs with graphics to enhance learning experiences.

TECHNOLOGY

138

Name_____ Date_____

CREATE A LIFELIKE CHARACTER

Duane Hanson and George Segal chose ordinary people as subjects for their artwork. The realism of the artists' work draws the viewer into the world of the sculptures.

WHAT TO DO: Create a story about the world of the sculptures in the lesson. Select one of the pieces and imagine what the life of the subject is like.

1. Describe the character you chose. Give him or her a name, occupation, age, family, and home. Use sensory descriptions and figurative language.

_____

_____

2. State a problem in the character's life.

_____

_____

3. Use the problem in a plot. Create suspense.
When does the character see the problem?
What steps does he or she take to solve it?
How do other characters help or cause problems?
What is the final solution?

_____

_____

_____

_____

4. On another sheet of paper, write a short story using the character and plot you have developed. Use dialogue. Write a final version of your story. Share it by reading it aloud, putting it in your classroom reading corner for others to read, or posting it on a bulletin board.

Reading/Language Arts Objective: The student produces engaging writing by using dialogue, suspense, figurative language.

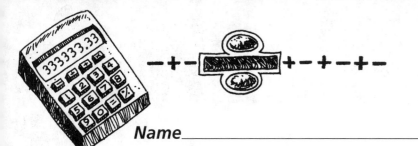

Name_____ Date_____

RATIO

Sculptors often begin by making a small model, called a *maquette,* of the work they are planning. Developing a large sculpture from the model involves careful use of ratio.

WHAT TO DO: Plan a realistic sculpture of a character from fiction for a permanent exhibit in your school library. Use the activities below to help you develop your sculpture.

1. Name and describe the character you want to show.

_____

_____

2. On another sheet of paper, sketch the character in the pose you want to use for your sculpture.

3. Write the measurements for your statue. For an adult, the height of the person should be about 7 heads; for a child, 5 or 6 heads. If your character is an animal, find a picture and work out the ratio of the head to body parts for that animal.

_____

_____

4. Work with a partner to figure out the length of your arms, legs, and body in "heads."

5. Decide on the height of the large statue you are planning. How many times larger is it than the model? Use that number to find the ratio of all parts. For example, if your statue is to be 6 feet tall and your model is 6 inches, you will work with a ratio of 12:1.

_____

_____

6. Make a final sketch of your statue. Mark each part of the drawing with the measurements you will need to make it realistic.

Mathematics Objective: The student uses ratio to describe the relationships between units of measure within the same measurement system.

Name _____ Date _____

HOME AND SCHOOL SAFETY

George Segal's people wait in safety for the green light. What safety procedures do you follow in a car? At home? At school?

WHAT TO DO: Answer the questions about the safety procedures that affect your life.

1. In 1966, Congress passed a law that allowed government agencies to require safety features on cars and trucks. What are some safety features that protect you when you ride in a car?

_____

_____

_____

2. Seat belts are required in all cars and most trucks. A seat belt is a strap—usually a combined shoulder and waist harness—that restrains an occupant in the seat, preventing him or her from being thrown forward during a sudden stop or change in direction. What conclusion can you draw from this requirement?

_____

_____

3. What are some procedures you observe at home to prevent fires?

_____

_____

_____

4. Think about sports you play in school or after school. List some safety procedures for a sport you enjoy.

_____

_____

_____

_____

Science Objective: The student observes and follows home and school safety procedures.

Name_____ Date_____

VASCO NÚÑEZ DE BALBOA, CONQUISTADOR

The scale and proportion a sculptor uses often provide interesting contrasts that can influence our thoughts on the subject.

WHAT TO DO: Show contrasting sides of a historical figure.

The Spanish conquistadors explored and conquered the Americas. They were usually more interested in wealth and fame than in governing or helping the people they conquered.

Vasco Núñez de Balboa was a conquistador who went to South America in 1501. He tried farming and failed. By 1510, he was in debt and stowed away on a ship to escape creditors.

On reaching Panama, Balboa crossed the isthmus and became the first European to see the eastern shore of the Pacific Ocean. His discovery encouraged the Spanish to explore and settle the western coast of South America.

1. Examine the drawing of Balboa. What makes him look heroic?

_____

_____

2. Draw a statue of Balboa as a new realist might portray him.

3. Find out more about Balboa's career as an explorer. List some

positive contributions he made._____

_____

4. List some actions by Balboa that were negative.

_____

_____

Social Studies Objective: The student researches and presents information on a leader from a specific time period.

SOCIAL STUDIES

Name_____ **Date**_____

ENCOUNTER WITH A SCULPTURE

The art of George Segal and Duane Hanson is part of a movement in art called new realism. Encountering sculptures in this style can be an interesting experience.

WHAT TO DO: Imagine a visitor to a museum coming upon a sculpture created by a new realist. Use pantomime to dramatize the event.

1. Plan the "meeting."

Where? _____

Who is the character? _____

What sculpture does the character "meet"? _____

_____

What reaction does the character show? _____

_____

Does the sculpture react? _____

2. Choose a mood.

Is the meeting scary? _____

Funny? _____

Other? _____

3. Write notes or an outline of the meeting.

_____

_____

_____

_____

4. Practice gestures, expressions, and body movements that will help you share what the meeting is like without using words.

5. Improvise the encounter for your class.

Arts (Theater) Objective: The student develops acting skills to develop characterizations that suggest artistic choices.

THE ARTS

Name_____ Date_____

Artists use scale and proportion to create life-size sculptures and then place them in realistic settings.

WHAT TO DO: Draw a person and place him or her in a familiar setting.

1. Select the 🖌 tool with a small brush or the 🖊 tool. Draw the whole body of someone you know. Use realistic proportions.

2. Select from a variety of tools. Draw a favorite place around your figure. Use a realistic scale.

3. Use the 🖊 tool, the 🖌 tool, or the ✍ tool to add visual texture, shading, and hues.

Technology Objective: The student uses software programs with graphics to enhance learning experiences.

144

Name_____ Date_____

BALANCE IN SENTENCES

An artwork is balanced when its lines, shapes, colors, and textures are distributed equally. In an artwork with formal balance, you can draw a line down the center and find the same elements on each side. You can also use balance in your sentences. Balance can emphasize contrast.

Many are called, but *few* are chosen.

The words *many* and *few* have opposite meanings—they balance against each other and form a contrast. Other times you can use words or phrases that match in some way to make your point.

The queen is as haughty as the king is greedy.

WHAT TO DO: Write the words that balance or match in each sentence. Where possible, draw a line dividing a sentence into two balanced halves.

1. You can take the mouse out of the country, but you can't take the

country out of the mouse. _____

2. Ask not what your country can do for you, rather ask what you can

do for your country. _____

3. He is all bark and no bite. _____

4. I cried because I had no shoes, until I met a man who had no feet.

_____

5. If March comes in like a lion, it will go out like a lamb.

_____

6. All work and no play makes Jack a dull boy. _____

7. Now, write a sentence with a balanced structure.

_____

Reading/Language Arts Objectives: The student writes in complete sentences varying sentence structure as appropriate. The student analyzes ways in which authors organize and present ideas to make text understandable.

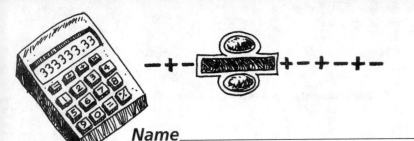

Name_____ Date_____

FLIPS, SLIDES, AND ROTATIONS

Cow's Skull: Red, White, and Blue has symmetry. Each half of the painting is a mirror image of the other. If you divided the image in half and flipped one half over onto the other, the halves would match. When figures have the same size and shape, they are **congruent**.

WHAT TO DO: Trace each shape in the left column. Cut out the shapes you traced. Slide, flip, and rotate each shape to find the congruent shape on the right.

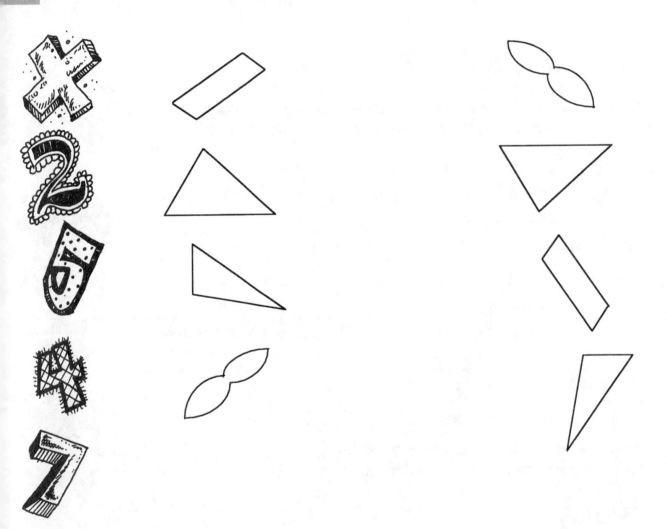

Mathematics Objective: The student uses translations, reflections, and rotations to make geometric patterns, using technology where appropriate.

Name _____ Date _____

FLOWER REPRODUCTION

In *Cow's Skull: Red, White, and Blue*, Georgia O'Keeffe uses symmetry. She also uses symmetry in many of her paintings of flowers. The form of a flower does not just make the flower pretty; it helps the flowering plant reproduce.

WHAT TO DO: Study the diagram and sentences about flower parts. Use the information to answer the questions.

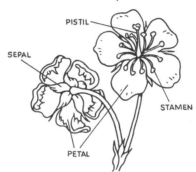

Sepals protect the unopened flower. *Petals* arranged in circles use color and *nectar* to attract pollinators (insects) that carry the pollen to other plants. *Stamens* produce *pollen* needed to reproduce. The *pistil* contains *ovules* (immature seeds). When pollen travels down the pistil and joins ovules, mature seeds form and are protected by a fruit.

1. The flower part that holds the seeds is the _____.

2. _____ produced by the stamens must get into the pistil for seeds to form.

3. This powdery substance travels from one flower to another on the

wings and feet of flower-visiting _____.

4. Butterflies and bees, for example, are drawn to flowers by the colors

of the _____ and the sweetness of the _____ .

5. Once the pollen travels down the _____ , the ovules are fertilized and seeds form.

6. Where the flower was, a _____ will form to protect the seeds.

Science Objective: The student examines interactions between organisms in an ecosystem that supports the organisms' survival.

Name_____ Date_____

ROBOTS AND SOCIETY

For this lesson, you designed a robot with symmetrical balance. Compare the robot you designed with the robot shown below.

WHAT TO DO: Study the picture of a robot and the information below. Then, answer the questions.

Robots are automatic machines that have changed society in many ways. A robot can do tasks quicker than a human, without getting bored or tired. Robots have made factories and businesses more productive. As more and more automatic and electronic machines have been introduced, many jobs once done by people have been taken over by machines. This has meant that people need more education to do jobs that require more skill. These jobs are likely to be more challenging and better paid than the jobs robots are doing.

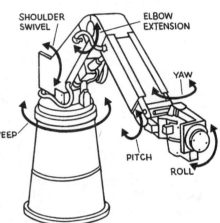

SHOULDER SWIVEL
ELBOW EXTENSION
YAW
ARM SWEEP
PITCH
ROLL

1. Explain what you think the robot does and how it does it. _____

_____

2. List three changes automatic machines have brought to people's lives in this century. _____

_____

_____

3. Imagine a robot that will do a job now done by humans. Name the robot and tell how it will change people's lives. _____

_____

Social Studies Objective: The student identifies and explains the changes in work patterns and economic activities in Texas and the United States.

SOCIAL STUDIES

Name _____ **Date** _____

ROBOT DANCE

The robot you made or are making for this project has symmetrical balance. Symmetrical balance works on a robot much as your two arms and legs help balance your body. Imagine the robot coming to life. How will it move?

WHAT TO DO: Experiment with different types of movements that you think a robot would make. Think about what the robot is made of and how it is put together. Answer the questions and follow the directions below.

1. Describe how the robot does each of the following:

    a. start moving: _____

    _____

    b. shift weight while walking: _____

    _____

    c. turn head: _____

    _____

    d. raise arms: _____

    _____

    e. stop: _____

    _____

2. Practice these movements as though you were a robot.
3. Invent a robot dance step. Use the movements you practiced. Keep your movements robotlike. Show symmetrical balance in your dance movements.

THE ARTS

Arts (Dance) Objective: The student demonstrates the following movement skills and explains the underlying principles: balance, initiation of movement, articulation of isolated body parts, weight shift, elevation and landing, fall and recovery.

Name_____ Date_____

Artists use formal balance to visually organize a work so that both sides match equally to create a pleasing mood. Symmetry is a type of formal balance in which the two halves are mirror images of each other.

WHAT TO DO: Draw a symmetrically balanced creature scene.

1. Use the  tool to draw an imaginary character.

Be sure to make both sides the same to create a symmetrically balanced creature. Use the Brush Mirrors command from the Options menu, if available.

Choose from a variety of brush thicknesses.

2. Draw a setting. Try to balance the background.

3. Add color to your scene. Think about the mood, and choose hues to match it.
Select from a variety of tools:

Technology Objective: The student uses software programs with graphics to enhance learning experiences.

TECHNOLOGY

150

Name_____ Date_____

CHANGES IN LANGUAGE

Just as styles of art have changed greatly over time, so has language. For example, the English language was much different in the time of Anguissola's painting than it is now. Many rules of grammar and spelling we use today did not exist.

WHAT TO DO: Read the stage directions written by William Shakespeare for the play *Hamlet*. Compare them with the version written in today's standard English. Underline differences and answer the questions.

Enter in a dumbe shew, the King and the Queene, he sits downe in an Arbor, she leaues him: Then, enters Lucianus with poyson in a Viall, and powres it in his ears, and goes away: Then, the Queen commeth and finds him dead. . . .

Enter in a dumb show, the king and the queen. He sits down in an arbor. She leaves him. Then, enters Lucianus with poison in a vial and pours it in his ears and goes away. Then, the queen comes and finds him dead. . . .

1. List five words that were spelled differently in Shakespeare's day. Beside them, write today's spelling.

_____

_____

_____

_____

_____

2. How does Shakespeare's use of capital letters differ from ours?

_____

_____

Reading/Language Arts Objectives: The student employs standard English usage. The student uses conventions such as capitalization and punctuation that clarify and enhance meaning.

Name_____   Date_____

FINDING AN UNKNOWN TO BALANCE AN EQUATION

In Anguissola's *The Chess Game*, figures and light and dark areas create informal balance. Although the figures and spaces on the left and right are not exactly the same, they seem equal. In a similar way, numbers and operations on each side of an equation may be different, yet they are equal.

$$29 + 21 = 32 + 18 \qquad \text{or} \qquad 37 - 12 = 12 + 13$$

WHAT TO DO: Write problems using addition and subtraction. Fill in the missing number and operation signs to make both sides equal, or balanced. Do each problem two ways.

A. 120 _____ 60 = 130 _____ _____

    120 _____ 60 = 130 _____ _____

B. 114 _____ _____ = 86 _____ _____

    114 _____ _____ = 86 _____ _____

C. _____ _____ 65 = 92 _____ _____

    _____ _____ 65 = 92 _____ _____

D. 110 _____ 70 = 90 _____ _____

    110 _____ 70 = 90 _____ _____

E. 96 _____ _____ = 189 _____ _____

    96 _____ _____ = 189 _____ _____

Mathematics Objective: The student uses addition and subtraction strategies to solve problems involving whole numbers.

152

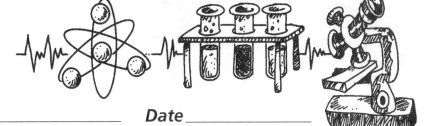

Name_____ **Date**_____

FORCE AND MOTION

In *Women of Paris, The Circus Lover*, two trapeze artists wait to perform. They will set the swings in motion by exerting a **force,** or a push. An object is at rest when opposite and equal forces are pushing on it. For example, a book rests on a table because the force of the table pushes the book up while the force of **gravity** pushes it down.

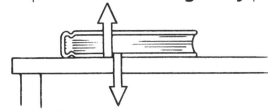

WHAT TO DO: A swing will move out and up in its path until the force of gravity becomes greater than the force pushing the swing and pulls the swing down. Predict what will happen next in each picture. Write your prediction on the lines beside the picture. Draw arrows to show the direction the figures will move.

1. _____

_____

_____

2. _____

_____

_____

3. _____

_____

_____

SCIENCE

Science Objective: The student explains the motion of objects as a result of the force applied.

Name _____ Date _____

MACHINES AND SOCIETY

The world of *The Chess Game* was quite different from the world of *Women of Paris, The Circus Lover*. In the 1700s and 1800s, the Industrial Revolution brought many changes to Europe. The invention of machines like the steam engine and the power loom changed the way things were made and the way people lived and worked.

For example, in Anguissola's Italy, cloth was woven slowly by hand. The weaver worked at home, which was usually in a quiet, rural place. In Tissot's France, cloth was produced quickly in factories on a power loom. Workers lived in the city and spent long hours running the machines.

WHAT TO DO: Read about important inventions below and answer the question.

1733 flying shuttle: one person could handle a wider loom more rapidly than two could before

1770 spinning jenny: one person could run eight spindles instead of one

1779 "mule": spinning machine used water power

1785 power loom: wove threads together by machine

1793 cotton gin: cleaned more cotton much faster

Explain how textile production changed from 1700 to 1800. Also explain how you think the lives of people changed because of the inventions.

_____

_____

_____

_____

_____

_____

Social Studies Objectives: The student describes how mass production and the Industrial Revolution affected economic growth. The student identifies changes in society that resulted from the Industrial Revolution.

154

SOCIAL STUDIES

Name _____ Date _____

CIRCUS CHARACTERS

In *Women of Paris, The Circus Lover,* Tissot has captured the exciting, exotic feel of the circus. Have you ever wondered what it would be like to perform in a circus? Do you have a favorite performer: lion tamer, elephant trainer, acrobat, bareback rider, clown? Imagine what a performance would be like from the point of view of one of these performers.

WHAT TO DO: Choose one circus performer and answer the following questions about him or her.

1. What sort of personality do you need to have to do your job?

_____

2. What actions and gestures go with your performance?

_____

_____

3. What do you like about being in front of the crowd?

_____

_____

4. How do you hold the audience's attention? How do you keep them

in suspense? _____

_____

_____

5. Now, write a brief description of your act. Include an action or episode that will cause tension in the audience.

_____

_____

_____

_____

_____

THE ARTS

Arts (Theater) Objective: The student creates characters, environments, and actions that create tension and suspense.

Name_____ Date_____

Artists use informal balance, also called asymmetry, to organize a design so that unlike objects have equal visual weight.

WHAT TO DO: Create a still life with informal balance.

1. Select the 🖌 tool or the ✏ tool. Draw several common objects. Use different colors.

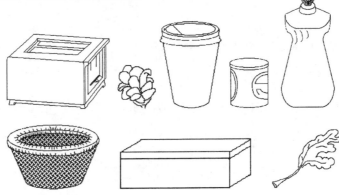

2. Select from a variety of tools: 🖌 ✏ 🏷 🔨 🗒
   Add textures, shading, and details to the objects.

3. Draw a table and background for the objects.

4. Use the 🖑 tool to arrange the objects on the table to create informal balance. Use one or more techniques to achieve this: size, color, texture, or position.

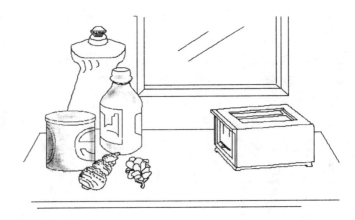

Technology Objective: The student uses software programs with graphics to enhance learning experiences.

TECHNOLOGY

Name _____ Date _____

EDITING A DRAFT

The designs on the dish and carpet in this lesson start in the center and repeat as they move away from the center. All the parts of the design connect to the center so that the entire design fits together.

In the same way, a piece of writing should connect to a topic sentence and fit together as a unit. You should **edit** your writing–analyze and change it–to be as clear and specific as possible. In addition to making sure all your ideas fit together, check each sentence. Make sure each sentence expresses a complete idea and is written correctly.

WHAT TO DO: Read the paragraph about functional art. Make sure each sentence supports the topic sentence. Correct any errors in spelling, punctuation, and grammar. Rewrite parts of sentences to improve them. Make your changes by writing above the line.

What gives an objet value as art? Does it have to be hanging on

the wall of a museum. Have to be expensiv? Sum people believe

that there is artistic beauty in common, ordinary objects around

us. For example, look around your kitchen. Look at a pitcher a

vase, and a bowl. They might be plain and humble, we can look

at them as works of art. In fact, their honest, straightforward

plainness makes them butiful. if their form is true to the function

they preform, they have value. Value that will stand the test of time.

Reading/Language Arts Objective: The student edits drafts for specific purposes (e.g., to ensure standard usage, varied sentence structure, etc.).

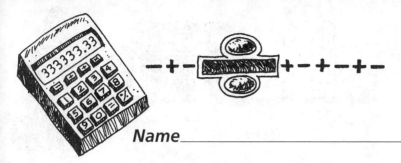

Name_____ Date_____

COMPLETING PATTERNS

Radial balance occurs when a pattern is repeated at least four times and radiates outward from a center point. You might see radial balance in something as simple as a dish. When you can see the elements used to create the pattern, you can complete an unfinished part of the pattern.

WHAT TO DO: In each design, supply the missing part of the pattern. First, show what makes the pattern by filling in the blanks. Then, draw the missing portion in the circle.

1.

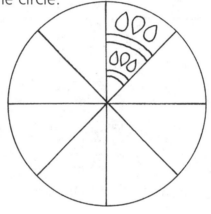

Pattern: 1_____ + 1_____ + 2_____ + 1_____

2.

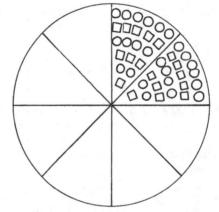

Pattern: 1_____ + 2_____ + 3_____ + 4_____ + 5_____

+ 6_____

Another way to say this is

"Count to seven. Odds =_____ and evens = _____ "

Mathematics Objectives: The student makes generalizations from patterns or sets of examples and nonexamples created with appropriate tools. The student selects an appropriate problem-solving strategy, including look for a pattern, etc.

Name_____ Date_____

RECORDING DATA ACCURATELY

Nature contains many kinds of balance. Flowers often show either radial or bilateral symmetry. If they have *radial symmetry*, they may be divided into two equal parts many different ways. Flowers with *symmetrical balance* can be divided into two equal parts only along one specific line.

WHAT TO DO: Observe the numbers of petals and stamens in each kind of flower. Record the data on the graph.

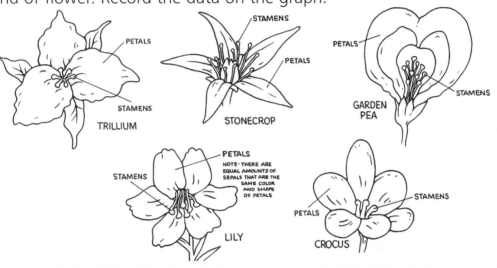

Flower	Number of Petals	Number of Stamens
stonecrop		
trillium		
garden pea		
lily		
crocus		

SCIENCE

Now, decide which statements you can support with the information above. Put an **X** beside each true statement.

_____ **1.** All flowers have petals in multiples of three.

_____ **2.** The number of stamens is two times the number of petals.

_____ **3.** The number of stamens is a multiple of the number of petals.

Science Objective: The student assesses accuracy of data collected from investigations.

Name _____ Date _____

COLONIAL FOLK ART—USEFUL THINGS

Like the carpet and the dish, folk art is made to be used. However, folk-art pieces are made by untrained artists and are usually simple and humble. Many of the items needed for daily life in colonial America were by craftspeople and family members, for there were no factories, there were few stores, and there was little money. Even though these objects were necessary, it was still important that they were beautiful.

WHAT TO DO: Read the information about each colonial item. On the line, write what the object was used for. Then, write who made it.

> cooper (barrel maker)   silversmith
> colonial woman   blacksmith

1. pewter cups, plates—This soft metal, made mostly of tin, was commonly used for utensils.

_____

2. quilts—Finely sewn patterns of pieced-together cloth made these essential blankets beautiful.

_____

3. iron pots—When heated until red-hot, iron could be hammered into various useful shapes.

_____

4. wooden casks—Curved strips of wood were held in place by metal strips to form these barrels.

_____

5. sampler—These small cloths showed off fancy needlework, featuring designs and letters.

_____

Social Studies Objective: The student interprets and analyzes historical social studies data.

SOCIAL STUDIES

Name _____ **Date** _____

FOLK SONGS

Functional art is made for everyday use. It is functional art that is simple and made by untrained artists. Folk songs were made up and passed along orally by people from generation to generation. A folk song expresses ideas and experiences with simple emotion and melody.

WHAT TO DO: Read the words and music of this folk song. It came to us from England and is over five hundred years old.

Riddle Song

"I gave my love a cher-ry that has no stone, I
gave my love a chick-en that has no bone, I
gave my love a gold ring that has no end, I
gave my love a ba-by with no cry-in.

1. With what feeling do you think "Riddle Song" should be sung?

_____

2. Study the words of "Riddle Song." It has repetitions, like a symmetrical work of art. Explain how its pattern is like radial balance.

_____

_____

_____

3. Sing the song.

Arts (Music) Objectives: The student compares in two or more arts how the characteristic materials of each art can be used to transform similar ideas into works of art. The student describes distinguishing characteristics of representative music genres and styles from a variety of cultures.

THE ARTS

Name_____ Date_____

Artists create radial balance, like spokes of a wheel, in artwork by repeating lines, shapes, and colors in a pattern that radiates from a center point.

WHAT TO DO: Create a design with radial balance.

1. Select the ▭ or ◯ shape tool. Draw a large geometric shape.

2. Use the 🖌 tool and a variety of colors to create a radially balanced design. Select the Brush Mirrors command from the Options menu, if available.

Find the center point by using the ruler. Start your design by creating a pattern all around the center point and then continue outward toward the edges of the shape.

Use a variety of shapes and line thicknesses.

3. You may wish to continue your patterns outside the shape outline or erase the outline with the ▱ tool.

Technology Objective: The student uses software programs with graphics to enhance learning experiences.

TECHNOLOGY

Name _____   Date_____

DESCRIBING FROM UP CLOSE, FROM FAR AWAY

Perspective techniques, such as those used in the paintings, let us see depth in flat paintings. For example, distinct colors and sharp, small details make an object seem close. You can indicate closeness or distance through your choice of words when writing a description. A close-up allows for great detail, while distance allows for a general impression.

WHAT TO DO: Read the describing sentences. Write **up close** or **distant** to show the perspective of the writer.

_____ **1.** A network of tiny blue veins stood out in the rough, wrinkled skin of his hands.

_____ **2.** The bus crawled like a yellow beetle on the dusty road, stopping now and then to drop off brightly colored specks of children.

_____ **3.** The yeasty smell of bread fresh from the oven, its brown crust gleaming with melted butter, made her feel faint with hunger.

_____ **4.** It started as a faint buzzing from the sky, gradually increasing until we could see the glinting wings of the biplanes in formation.

Now, write two descriptions of a familiar object: one close-up and one distant. Use details that make your perspective clear.

up close: _____

_____

_____

far away: _____

_____

_____

Reading/Language Arts Objectives: The student writes to inform (describe). The student reads to appreciate the writer's craft, to become informed, to discover models for one's own writing.

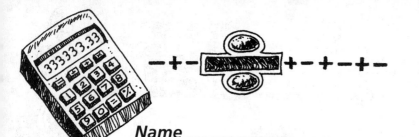

Name_____ Date_____

READING A SCHEDULE

Monet's impression of the busy train station in Paris is full of light, energy, and movement. Trains run on a schedule. Commuters depend on trains to get them where they need to be on time. Reading a train schedule is a necessary skill.

WHAT TO DO: Frank lives in Holly. Read the train schedule to decide which trains Frank must take to make his appointments.

Leaving Holly	6:45 A.M.	7:45 A.M.	9:45 A.M.	11:15 A.M.	12:45 P.M.	2:45 P.M.	– –	5:15 P.M.
Arriving Metropolis	7:30 A.M.	9:00 A.M.	10:30 A.M.	12 NOON	1:30 P.M.	3:30 P.M.	– –	6:00 P.M.
Leaving Metropolis	8:00 A.M.	10:00 A.M.	–	12 NOON	–	4:00 P.M.	5:00 P.M.	6:00 P.M.
Arriving Holly	9:00 A.M.	11:00 A.M.	–	1:15 P.M.	–	5:00 P.M.	6:15 P.M.	7:00 P.M.

1. Frank works at Bond Brothers' store in Metropolis. He starts work at 9:45 A.M. It takes fifteen minutes to get to the store from the Metropolis train station. What train must he take from Holly?

_____

2. Frank gets out of work at 4:15. When will he get to Holly? _____

3. Frank has a doctor's appointment in Holly at 3 P.M. What train will

he have to take home to make this appointment? _____

4. On a vacation day, Frank goes to the 2:00 baseball game in Metropolis. The game should be over by 5:30 P.M. The stadium is 20 minutes from the Metropolis train station. Can he take the train?

_____

Mathematics Objective: The student describes everyday situations using mathematical language and symbols.

164

Level 5, Unit 5, Lesson 4
ART CONNECTIONS:
*The Arrival of the Normandy Train
at the Gare Saint-Lazare*

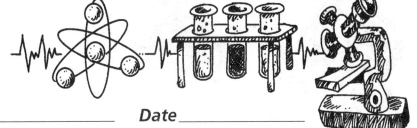

Name _____ Date _____

STEAM POWER

Monet painted great clouds of steam around the train in *The Arrival of the Normandy Train.* The steam locomotive made use of the energy of steam to turn wheels. Steam is the gas form of water. Water is turned into steam by adding heat energy. The energy of steam can be harnessed to do work.

WHAT TO DO: Use the diagram to answer the questions. Write **true** if the statement is true; write **false** if the statement is false.

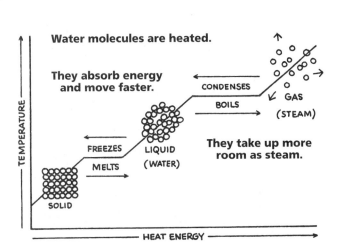

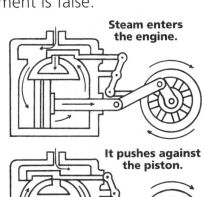

Steam enters the engine.

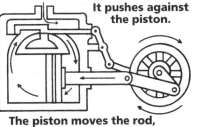

It pushes against the piston.

The piston moves the rod, which moves the flywheel.

_____ **1.** Molecules of water are closer together than molecules of steam.

_____ **2.** Molecules of water have more energy than molecules of steam.

_____ **3.** Steam can exert a force to move objects.

_____ **4.** Steam molecules move more rapidly than water molecules.

_____ **5.** In a steam engine, only the piston moves.

_____ **6.** In a steam engine, steam forces the piston to move.

_____ **7.** In a steam engine, the energy of steam is used to create energy of movement.

Science Objectives: The student conducts investigations related to the phases of matter. The student analyzes a model to show that changes in the speed or direction of motion are caused by forces.

Name _____ Date _____

TRANSPORTING PEOPLE

Monet's painting helps us imagine what it was like to travel by train in 1877 when the steam locomotive was a relatively new invention. For centuries, people had traveled overland largely by wagon, carriage, or stagecoach. The train, although it had its discomforts and dangers, transported more people in a faster, more efficient way.

WHAT TO DO: Imagine yourself a traveler on the steam locomotive in Monet's painting. Use details from the painting and your own store of knowledge to answer the questions.

_____ **1.** The train might reach a top speed of (a) 10 mph (b) 25 mph (c) 70 mph (d) 130 mph.

_____ **2.** For fuel to heat water, the steam locomotive used (a) coal (b) gasoline (c) electricity (d) uranium.

_____ **3.** The seating on the train was (a) comfortable (b) luxurious (c) uncomfortable (d) spacious.

_____ **4.** The passenger cars pulled by the engine were (a) unheated and smelled of burning coal (b) much like a wagon (c) air conditioned and heated (d) equipped with eating and sleeping facilities.

Invent a new form of transportation for the twenty-first century. Answer the questions about your invention.

5. In the twenty-first century, we will travel by _____ .

6. This invention will use_____ power to move millions of people.

7. Here is a description of my people mover: _____

_____

_____

8. On the back of this paper, draw your people mover. Tell how it will change people's lives.

Social Studies Objective: The student predicts changes that may occur in the future as a result of new technology.

SOCIAL STUDIES

Name _____   Date _____

DEVELOPING A CHARACTER

The guide whose house Arthur Lismer painted was an Algonquin living in the Canadian wilds. What do the setting and the house suggest about the guide? What was his life like?

Character is established by what a person looks like, says, and does. A straight posture and neat appearance suggest pride, for example. Giving away possessions to someone in need suggests compassion and generosity.

WHAT TO DO: Picture the Algonquin guide outside his house. You have come to hire him. Fill in his character with the following details.

1. Describe the guide. _____

_____

_____

2. Describe his clothing and shoes. _____

_____

_____

3. How does he feel about his home? _____

_____

4. How does he move? _____

_____

5. How does he treat his horse? _____

_____

On the back of this page, draw a picture of the character you created. Let facial expression, posture, and costume show personality. Write an opening dialogue between you and the guide. Read another student's character analysis and dialogue. Take turns acting out the scene.

Arts (Theater) Objectives: The student refines and records dialogue and action. The student analyzes descriptions, dialogue, and actions to discover character motivation and invent character behaviors based on the observation of interactions, ethical choices, and emotional responses of people.

167

THE ARTS

Name_____ Date_____

Artists use perspective techniques to create depth on a flat surface so that some objects look close and others look far away.

WHAT TO DO: Create a peaceful landscape scene using perspective techniques.

1. Close your eyes and think of a peaceful setting. Draw the objects you might find there.
Select several colors and a variety of tools:

2. Select your objects with the 🖋 tool or the ⬚ tool, and arrange them to show perspective. Change the size of some objects and overlap them. Move smaller shapes higher on the screen.

3. Add more features to the scene.

4. Add details. Use clear, sharp details for the objects that will appear up close.

5. Fill the scene with color. Think of the mood and add colors to match. Choose colors that look like they fade in the distance. Select from a variety of tools:

Technology Objective: The student uses software programs with graphics to enhance learning experiences.

TECHNOLOGY

168

Name _____ Date _____

FARM JOURNAL

What would it be like to spend a day on the Cornell Farm? In 1848, life on a farm meant daily hard work for everyone in the family. Much of a family's food was raised there. There was no electricity, gas, engine-powered vehicles, or running water.

Then, as now, a person might keep a diary or journal of daily events. Writing about events is often done in *chronological order*. This means you tell what happened first, second, third, and so on in time order.

WHAT TO DO: Imagine that you have spent a day on Cornell Farm. Write in your journal what you did, what happened, and how you felt about your experiences. Put events in chronological order, from daybreak until bedtime.

Date: _____

_____

_____

_____

_____

_____

_____

_____

_____

_____

_____

_____

_____

_____

Reading/Language Arts Objectives: The student writes to inform (e.g., report, narrate). The student chooses the appropriate form for his or her purpose for writing.

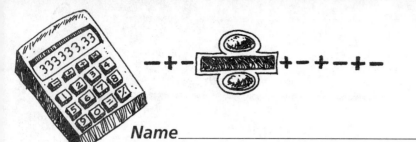

Name_____   Date_____

GARDEN FRACTIONS

The large farm Edward Hicks painted raised crops and livestock. The United States was built on farming. Today, for enjoyment and health, many Americans still raise a small garden. Planning is required, whether the garden covers 1,500 acres or a small fraction of that.

WHAT TO DO: Complete Mr. Cornell's garden plan, using information in item 1 below. Then, use the plan to solve the problems.

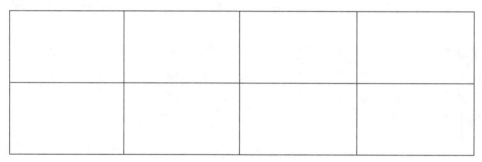

1. Each section of the garden has three rows or four hills. Fill in the eight sections with the crops listed.
   corn–6 rows   tomatoes–6 rows
   peas–3 rows   lettuce and radishes–3 rows
   pumpkins and squash–4 hills each
2. Name the fraction of the garden taken up by each food.

   corn _____ tomatoes _____

   peas _____ lettuce and radishes _____

   pumpkins and squash _____
3. What two foods make up half the garden?

   _____

4. What fraction of the garden is lettuce, radishes, and peas? _____
5. Each hill of pumpkins will have 5 seeds. A packet contains 25 seeds.

   Does Mr. Cornell have enough? _____
6. Mr. Cornell will plant 20 kernels of corn in each row. How many

   kernels of corn must he buy? _____

Mathematics Objectives: The student uses concrete and pictorial models to add and subtract fractions with like denominators in problem-solving situations. The student selects and uses multiplication facts, strategies, etc., to solve problems involving whole numbers.

Name_____   **Date**_____

A CHANGING LANDSCAPE

In Edward Hicks's painting, we see the farm as it was 150 years ago. What would it look like today? Over time, the land changes due to erosion and use. Inventions and new technology mean changes in buildings, machinery, and methods of farming. Growth in population means increases in the number of people using the land.

WHAT TO DO: Predict how the farm in the painting has changed in 150 years. Write two sentences describing each kind of change.

Land Changes: _____

_____

_____

Changes in the Use of Land: _____

_____

_____

Changes in Buildings: _____

_____

_____

Changes in Machinery and Technology: _____

_____

_____

Changes in Population and Neighbors: _____

_____

_____

On the back of this paper, draw a picture showing the landscape of the Cornell Farm today. Sketch in the general form of the land. Then, draw in new buildings, different machinery, different uses of the land, and so on.

Science Objective: The student compares and contrasts actions and events in which changes have occurred over time.

Name_____ Date_____

ARCHITECTURAL AND CULTURAL VALUES

The buildings represented in the two paintings of this lesson are quite different. The Roman basilica combines elements of church and royal splendor. The farm buildings are simple and plain. The buildings a society puts up express something about what that culture values, or thinks important.

WHAT TO DO: Select words from the word bank that describe the architecture in each painting. Write them beneath the appropriate headings. You might want to use some of the words and phrases in both descriptions.

grand	intricate	practical	angular
arched	luxurious	plain	simple
wooden	stone	sculpted	ornate
enormous	just big enough	for people	for animals
beautiful	expensive		

ST. PETER'S	CORNELL FARM

Choose one of the artworks. Explain what values you think the type of building or buildings shown expresses.

_____

_____

_____

Social Studies Objective: The student identifies various ways that architecture, beliefs, and values contributed to the development and transmission of culture in the United States.

Name _____ Date _____

SONGS REFLECT SOCIETIES

Hicks's painting shows a peaceful farm in the northeastern United States during the late 1840s. At the time, some farms like this one served as stations, or resting spots, on the Underground Railroad. Slaves escaping on the Underground Railroad used the song "Follow the Drinking Gourd" as a guide to moving north. The drinking gourd was another name for the Big Dipper, a group of stars that points to the North Star.

WHAT TO DO: Read the words to the refrain of "Follow the Drinking Gourd." Then, complete the activity.

> Follow the drinking gourd,
> Follow the drinking gourd,
> For the old man is a-waiting
> For to carry you to freedom,
> Follow the drinking gourd.

1. What advice does the refrain give? _____

_____

_____

2. Why would an escaping slave have followed that advice? _____

_____

_____

3. Write a verse to the song that gives directions that might have helped an escaping slave on the Underground Railroad.

_____

_____

_____

_____

4. Think of a tune that you can use for the song. Sing the refrain and your lyrics for "Follow the Drinking Gourd."

Arts (Music) Objective: The student compares, in several cultures of the world, functions music serves, roles of musicians, and conditions under which music is typically performed.

THE ARTS

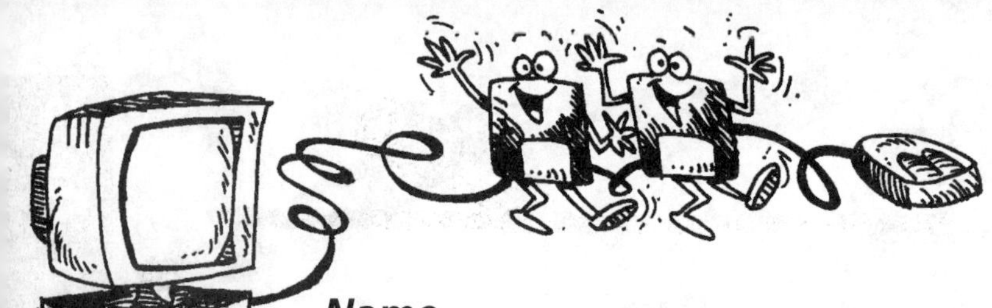
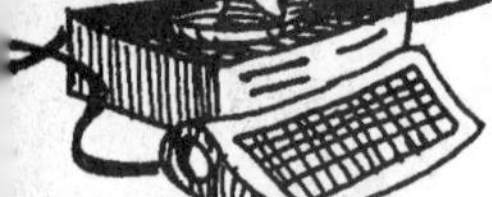

Name ______________________________ **Date** ______________

Artists use linear perspective techniques to show distance and depth in artwork.

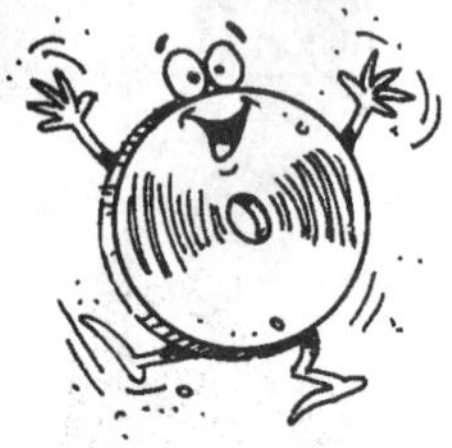

WHAT TO DO: Draw a scene using linear perspective techniques.

1. Use the tool to draw a horizon line across the page. Use the tool to draw a dot for a vanishing point.

2. Draw a simple house outline above and below the horizon line. Use the tool while holding down the Shift key to ensure straight vertical and horizontal lines. Draw lines in a light color from the top and bottom edges of the house shape to the vanishing point.

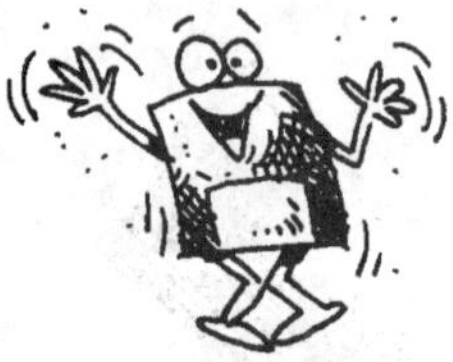
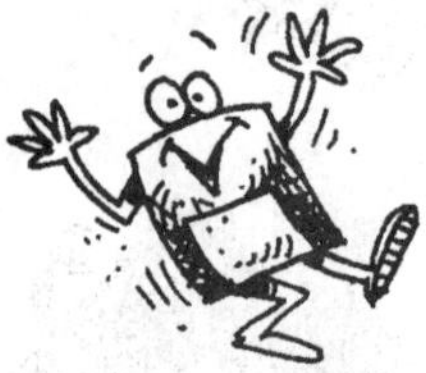

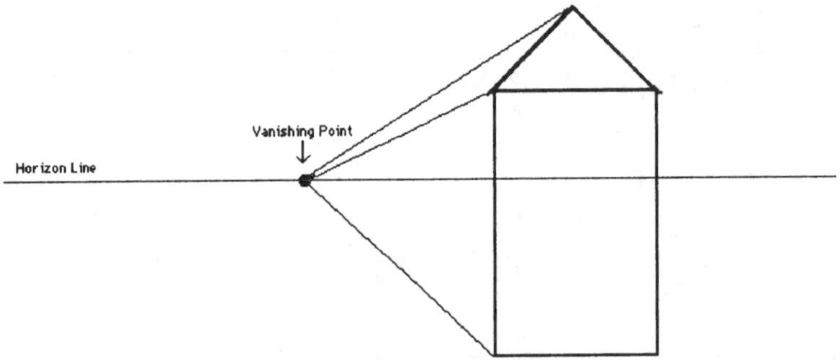

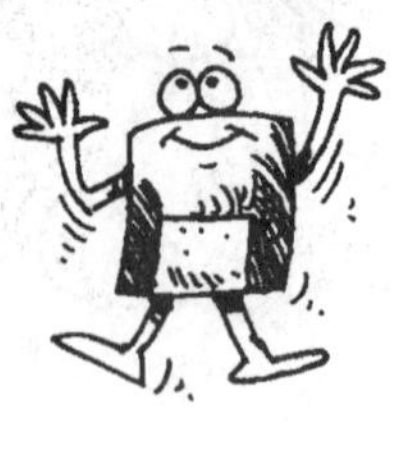

3. Add details to the house. Use the vanishing point to guide the top and bottom lines of windows, chimneys, doors, and roofs.

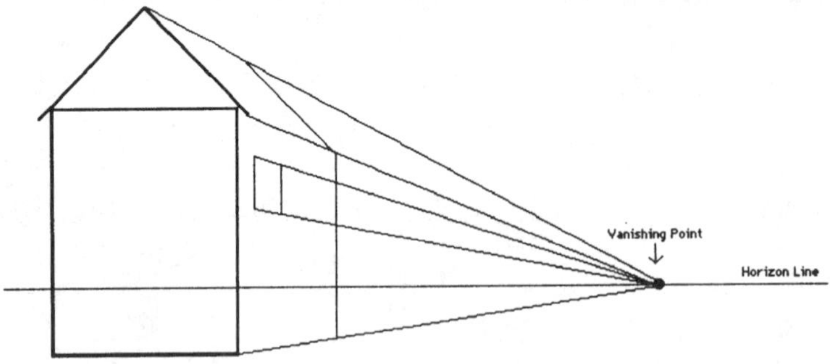

4. Add free-form shapes. Use overlapping and varying detail to show depth. Remember to place smaller objects higher up on the screen.
Imagine guidelines along the top and bottom of each object leading to the vanishing point. Draw the guidelines if you need them to help you.

TECHNOLOGY

Technology Objective: The student uses software programs with graphics to enhance learning experiences.

Name_____ **Date**_____

POINT OF VIEW IN A STORY

From what perspective do you view Sheeler's room and Hopper's house? Point of view is vital because it controls how we see. In a story, the storyteller controls how you view a story. A story told from the point of view of a lost child will differ greatly from the same story told by the parent searching for the child.

WHAT TO DO: Imagine that objects in the paintings can speak. What is the point of view of each one? Write a sentence answering the question as if you were the object.

House by the Railroad

1. The house: How do you feel about the trains passing by? _____

_____

_____

2. The train tracks: How do you feel about the house standing so close

by?_____

_____

_____

American Interior (imagine it is a potter's room)
3. The mug: How do you feel about the potter who made you and uses

you every day? _____

_____

_____

4. The vase: How do you feel about having no pattern, while the

saucers, the mug, and even the rugs have patterns? _____

_____

_____

Reading/Language Arts Objective: The student writes to express emotions, to develop and record ideas, and to reflect. The student writes to entertain self and others.

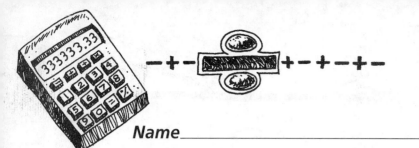

Name_____ Date_____

IDENTIFYING FORMS FROM DIFFERENT ANGLES

Charles Sheeler's *American Interior* provides an overhead view. The viewer is looking down into the room. Forms appear three-dimensional. The artist must use geometric forms and shading to make objects appear solid. Forms look different from different points of view.

WHAT TO DO: Identify each geometric form on the first line. On the second line, write the point of view from which the form is viewed: *front, side, back, overhead.*

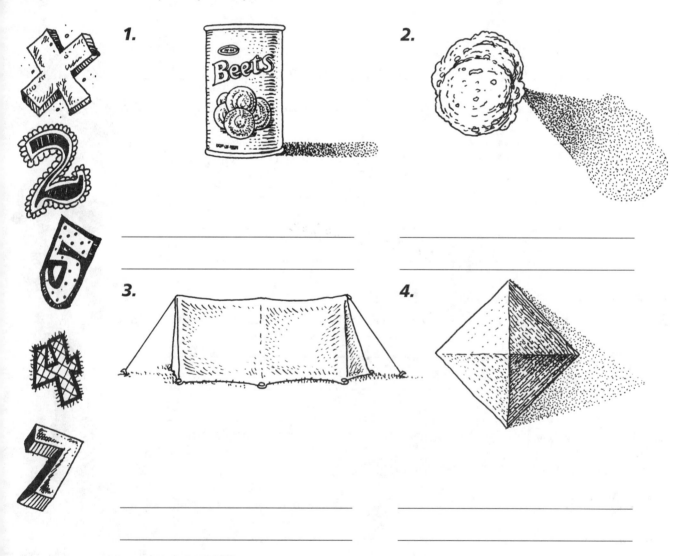

1.

_____

_____

2.

_____

_____

3.

_____

_____

4.

_____

_____

Mathematics Objective: The student identifies the critical attributes of geometric shapes of solids.

176

Name _____ Date _____

SAFE LEVELS OF SOUND

Hopper's house by the railroad appears to be very close to the tracks. What a commotion there must be when a train goes by! The windows vibrate, the floors shake, and the noise is terrific.

Sound is a form of energy that travels in waves. The amount of energy in a sound wave is its intensity. Sound intensity is measured in *decibels*. Sounds of 10 decibels are so soft you can barely hear them. Sounds of 120 or more decibels are painful. Listening to sounds of 85 decibels over long periods can damage one's ears.

WHAT TO DO: Study the table. On the lines below it, list similar sounds and write the decibel range into which you would place them. Put a * beside any sounds that could damage your ears.

Sound	Decibels	Sound	Decibels
whisper	10-20	heavy traffic	70-80
soft music	30	vacuum cleaner	75-85
classroom	35	loud music	90-100
conversation	60-70	jet engine	170

_____ _____ _____ _____

_____ _____ _____ _____

Study the table and answer the questions.

1. What sound is very painful to human ears? _____

2. Which sounds could damage your ears? _____

_____

3. Why do ground crews at airports wear special ear protection?

_____

4. Keep a diary of the noises you hear in one day. List the noises over 70 decibels. Do you think your hearing is at risk? If so, how can you

protect it? _____

_____

Science Objective: The student differentiates between sound pollution and safe sound levels.

Name_____ Date_____

RAILROADS AND U. S. EXPANSION

The tracks of the *House by the Railroad* seem to be the house's sole contact with society. While the United States was growing in the 1800s, railroads were an important link between communities. In the Midwest and West, the train brought new settlers, goods, and supplies from the East.

WHAT TO DO: Use the bar graph and history to answer the questions below.

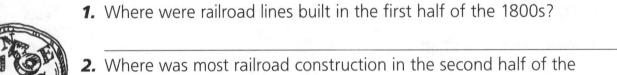

1830	
1831 - 1849	
1850 - 1860	
1880 - 1890	

0   500   1000   1500   2000   2500   3000   3500   4000   4500   5000   5500   6000   6500   7000

Miles of new railroad track construction per year

1830 - First stretch of rail transit opens
1848 - 6,000 miles of railway connect Atlantic states
1849 - Gold Rush in California creates demand for a transcontinental railroad
1862 - Government grants land to railroad companies
1869 - First transcontinental railroad complete

1. Where were railroad lines built in the first half of the 1800s?

_____

2. Where was most railroad construction in the second half of the

1800s? _____

3. When did the rate of construction grow the most? _____

4. How do you think the transcontinental railroads affected the

economy in the late 1800s? _____

_____

Social Studies Objective: The student uses geographic tools to organize, interpret, and share information about people, places, events, and the environment. The student summarizes the changing effects of migration, transportation, communication, military action, and technological innovations on the economic growth of Texas and the United States.

SOCIAL STUDIES

Name _____ **Date** _____

RAILROAD SONGS

The words, music, and rhythms of some American songs grow out of the workplace or an era in history. Some of these songs describe the characteristics of a place. What kind of song would Americans have written about Hopper's house by the railroad?

WHAT TO DO: Answer the following questions.

1. Look at these titles.
"I've Been Working on the Railroad"
"Wabash Cannonball"
"Chattanooga Choo-Choo"
"The Railroad Runs Through the Middle of the House"

What do they have in common? _____

_____

2. Explain why "I've Been Working on the Railroad" has a strong rhythm and upbeat tempo.

_____

_____

_____

3. Now, think of a song you know that has a good railroad rhythm. Use this melody and rhythm as the basis for your own song about the house by the railroad. Write at least one stanza, or verse, on the lines.

_____

_____

_____

_____

_____

Arts (Music) Objectives: The student compares, in several cultures of the world, functions music serves, roles of musicians, and conditions under which music is typically performed. The student analyzes the uses of elements of music in aural examples representing diverse genres and cultures.

THE ARTS

Name_____ Date_____

Artists create scenes using different points of view.

WHAT TO DO: Draw an indoor or outdoor scene from two different points of view.

1. Select from a variety of tools: 🖌 ✏ 🪣 ▭ ◯ ➘
Draw an indoor or outdoor scene from one viewpoint.

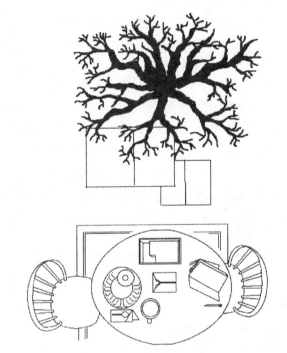

2. Draw the same scene from a different point of view.

3. Use the 🖌 tool or the ✏ tool to add shadows to each scene. Show the effects of light from two different perspectives.

Technology Objective: The student uses software programs with graphics to enhance learning experiences.

TECHNOLOGY

Name_____ Date_____

CONTRASTS IN LANGUAGE

In art, contrast is used to emphasize objects and actions. In language, words and phrases with contrasting meanings and feelings emphasize ideas. For example, a clean room might contain *sparkling linoleum floors, spotless chairs,* and *freshly painted walls.* Your attention would be drawn immediately to a *grimy, filthy window* in that room.

WHAT TO DO: In each group of words or phrases, circle the contrasting item. Use a dictionary if you are not sure of meaning.

1. sugary, acidic, sour, lemony
2. success, well-being, distress, abundance
3. explore, cover up, investigate, nose around
4. golden sunshine, wintry blast, Indian summer, picking apples
5. gentle breeze, parching thirst, rippling waves, warm sand
6. crowded sidewalk, bumper-to-bumper traffic, towering skyscrapers, quiet pond

Write two sentences in which you set up a contrast in order to call attention to an object or event.

7. _____

_____

8. _____

_____

Reading/Language Arts Objective: The student writes to inform.

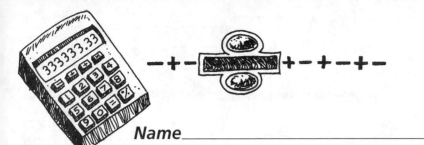

Name_____ Date_____

GRID LOCATION AND EMPHASIS IN A DESIGN

In Anne Beard's *Rodeo Jacket*, the cowboy with the lariat and the horse he is about to lasso are emphasized. A white outline and the color and placement cause you to look at these figures first. The location of pieces in an appliquéd artwork also creates interest and focus. You can use a *coordinate grid* to experiment with placement of pieces in a design.

WHAT TO DO: Here is a design for a wall hanging. Study the placement of its parts. Use the grid number system to give the location of the center of each shape.

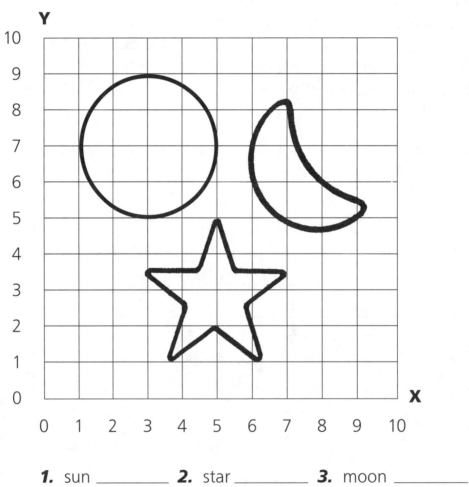

1. sun _____ **2.** star _____ **3.** moon _____

Mathematics Objective: The student uses ordered pairs of whole numbers to locate or name points on a coordinate grid.

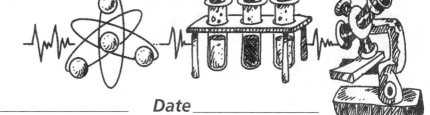

Name _____ Date _____

IDENTIFYING CLOUDS AND PREDICTING WEATHER

A contrast shows a difference. It makes something stand out. Different kinds of clouds that form in the atmosphere look quite different. Each kind indicates coming changes in weather. By learning to identify these contrasting types of clouds, you can predict weather.

WHAT TO DO: Study each cloud type. Answer the questions below about clouds and weather.

Cumulus clouds form in fluffy heaps as warm air rises. They indicate fair weather.

Cirrus clouds are high, thin, and cold. They indicate fair weather.

Stratus clouds spread out in layers where a large air mass rises slowly. They bring rain.

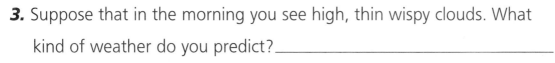

1. Write the name of the cloud that fits each description.

a. thin and feathery _____

b. high and puffy _____

c. layered and low _____

2. List the cloud types in order, from lowest to highest.

_____

3. Suppose that in the morning you see high, thin wispy clouds. What

kind of weather do you predict?_____

4. Then, in the afternoon, it gets warmer and layers of low-lying clouds

move in. What weather change can you predict? _____

_____

Science Objective: The student predicts outcomes after gathering and measuring data that show change.

Name _____ Date _____

THE RODEO AND WESTERN CULTURE

The rodeo jacket, like the rodeo itself, celebrates the life of the cowhand. Rodeos helped define Western culture.

WHAT TO DO: Read the information about rodeos. Underline parts that connect rodeos to cattle ranching. On another sheet of paper, write a paragraph explaining the relationship between rodeos and cattle ranching in your own words.

Rodeos are contests of skill and strength that grew out of cattle ranching, and rodeo events are related to everyday ranching activities. Rodeos began in the 1800s during annual roundups of cattle. (The word *rodeo* originally meant "roundup" in Spanish.) When cowhands drove herds to market, they would celebrate by holding competitions. They would exhibit their skills in bronco riding, bull riding, calf roping, and steer wrestling. By the 1880s, rodeos grew to be formal competitions for prize money, with paying audiences in attendance.

In the riding events, a contestant mounts a bull or horse confined in a chute. When released, the animal bolts and tries to buck the rider, who must remain mounted for a set time—usually 8 to 10 seconds. In steer wrestling, the contestant, on horseback, tries to corner a running steer and throw it to the ground. As the horse overtakes the steer, the contestant slides off the horse, grasps the horns of the steer and wrenches its horns until it falls to the ground. The contestant who does this quickest wins the event.

In calf roping, the contestant and cowpony work as a team to pursue the calf, lasso it, yank it to a halt, and tie its feet together. Again, speed decides the winner.

Social Studies Objective: The student identifies ways that traditions, values, and behaviors contributed to the development and transmission of culture in Texas and the United States.

Name_____ Date_____

CREATING CONTRAST IN DANCE

The Ponca blouse pictured in the lesson might have been worn for a ritual dance. Dance involves movement of the body and feet in rhythm to music. To add interest, a dance may contain contrasting kinds of movement or contrasting shapes made with the body. For example, quick hopping movements contrast with slow gliding movements.

WHAT TO DO: Imagine that you are a Ponca. Invent a dance for your coming-of-age celebration (showing you are now a young adult). Describe two contrasting steps and movements in your dance. Explain the contrasting emotions or stages that they show.

1. _____

_____

_____

2. _____

_____

_____

3. _____

_____

_____

Teach your dance to someone else, and practice it together. Think of new ways to combine contrasting movements and shapes as you dance together. Perform your dance for the class.

THE ARTS

Arts (Dance) Objectives: The student clearly demonstrates the principles of contrast and transition. The student demonstrates partner skills in a visually interesting way: creating contrasting and complementary shapes, etc.

Name_____ Date_____

Artists use color, shape, size, and location to emphasize or draw attention to an area in an artwork.

WHAT TO DO: Create a personal logo design with emphasis.

1. Select from a variety of tools:
Create a design with simple lines and shapes. Explore turning and inverting your initials.

2. Use the ⌐⌐ tool to select your design. Choose the Copy and Paste commands from the Edit menu to create multiple copies. Choose commands from the Selection menu to rotate some of the designs and combine the lines and shapes to make a logo that could be used on clothing.

3. Use the ⌐⌐ tool to select your logo and create copies.

4. Arrange the logos into a design and color it with the 🖌 tool. Create emphasis in the design with size, shape, or color.

Technology Objective: The student uses software programs with graphics to enhance learning experiences.

TECHNOLOGY

Name _____ **Date** _____

THE FOCUS OF A PARAGRAPH

The focal point of a painting is something like the topic sentence of a paragraph. Both create a focus. A *topic sentence* presents the main idea of a paragraph. It states the topic and your point of view about that topic. All other sentences present details about the topic.

WHAT TO DO: Find and underline the topic sentence in each paragraph. Notice its location.

   Crows are unusually sociable animals. They meet in large congregations at a common assembly ground. The birds fly to roosting trees where they line up in rows on the branches. Such a communal roost may contain hundreds of the birds. They are even sociable when hunting. In early morning, they take flight together, flying in long lines to forage for food.
   Crows can be tamed if taken from the nest when young. Some have even been taught to talk. Their curiosity and intelligence make them both interesting and entertaining. For example, many crows will take and hoard objects that interest them. You may never have thought of having a crow as a pet, but they can make good ones.

Now, write a paragraph about something that interests you. Exchange paragraphs with a classmate. Find your classmate's topic sentence.

_____

_____

_____

_____

_____

_____

_____

_____

Reading/Language Arts Objective: The student recognizes a text's main ideas and how those ideas are supported with details.

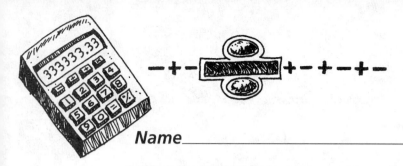

Name_____ Date_____

MEASUREMENTS AND CALCULATIONS TO STRING A LOOM

To make a loom like the one pictured in this lesson, you must figure out how many warp threads are needed, how long each should be, and how much extra thread will be needed to tie off each one. By measuring and using simple math, you can string a loom accurately.

WHAT TO DO: Study the loom. Count, measure, and calculate to answer the questions. Show your work.

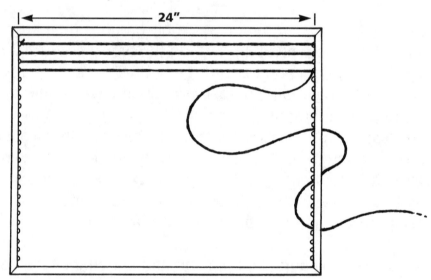

1. When the loom is warped, there will be _____ warp threads.

2. Each warp thread extends_____ inches.

3. Allow 6 inches on each end of a warp thread to have room to tie it

   off. How long should each warp thread be?_____

4. How many feet of thread must you purchase to string all the warp

   threads?_____

5. You find spools of thread that contain 25 yards, 50 yards, and 75

   yards. Which spool should you buy?_____

Mathematics Objectives: The student uses multiplication and division strategies to solve problems involving whole numbers. The student uses measurement procedures to solve problems involving length.

Name _____ Date _____

CHARACTERISTICS OF WOOL

Wool is the fleece of sheep. It is used to make thread and yarn for weaving. Why is it so highly prized for these uses?

WHAT TO DO: Study the structure of wool. Use the information to explain the characteristics of wool.

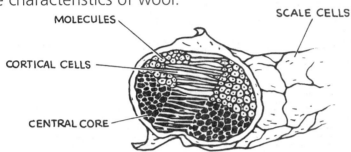

Scale cells cover the outer surface of each fiber. They allow fibers to interlock under pressure.

Cortical cells have elasticity. They allow fibers to stretch and return to original shape.

Central core has air spaces. These make wool light and increase its insulating power.

Molecules that make up wool are folded upon each other many times. When a wool fiber is stretched, the molecules unfold. When the fiber is released, they spring back to their natural position. The molecules are also bulky, which makes wool highly absorbent.

1. What makes wool fabric tight and warm? _____

_____

2. Why does wool keep its shape even after many wearings?

_____

_____

3. Why does wool insulate well? _____

_____

_____

Science Objective: The student applies his or her knowledge of the properties of matter to solve a design problem.

Name _____ Date _____

CHANGES IN THE NAVAJO CULTURE

The Navajo are native to the American Southwest. Many years ago, they were hunters who moved around to find food. Later, they lived by herding sheep, moving their herds to new pastures as needed throughout the year. A rounded mud-and-wood structure called a *hogan* served as home at each grazing site. Today, the Navajo are well known for their woven wool blankets and rugs and their beautiful silver and turquoise jewelry. The culture of the Navajo today is completely different from their original culture. How did it change so much?

WHAT TO DO: Study these events. On the lines provided, write a paragraph giving some reasons the Navajo culture changed from hunting and wandering to herding and producing goods.

1300-1600	Migrated from Canada into the Arizona and New Mexico region; were hunters and nomads; made frequent war raids on the Pueblo
by 1600	Learned from the Pueblo to plant corn, beans, and squash in large fields; from Spaniards, got horses and learned to raise sheep for meat and wool
by 1800	Navajo blankets and ponchos in great demand
by 1850	Learned from Mexicans to make silver jewelry

_____

_____

_____

_____

_____

_____

_____

_____

Social Studies Objective: The student compares and contrasts ways that groups during the development of Texas and the United States met their basic needs.

Name _____   Date _____

EMPHASIS IN MUSIC

Emphasis makes something stand out from its surroundings. Color, location, or shape may accomplish this in an artwork. In music, notes may be emphasized in several ways. These signs placed over or under notes direct a musician to give different kinds of emphasis.

staccato	•	make the note short and sharp, separation between each note
crescendo	*cresc.*	gradually become louder
diminuendo	➤	gradually become softer
forte	*f*	loudly
piano	*p*	softly

WHAT TO DO: Read the following passage of music. Beside the number that matches each measure, explain the kind of emphasis that should be given.

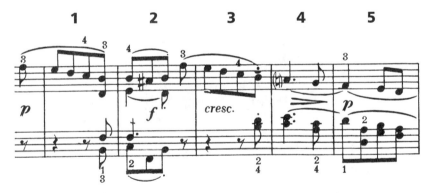

1. _____

2. _____

3. _____

4. _____

5. _____

THE ARTS

Arts (Music) Objective: The student describes specific music events in a given aural example, using appropriate terminology.

Name_____ Date_____

Artists use lines, shapes, colors, size, and placement to emphasize or draw attention to an area in an artwork. This is called the center of interest, or focal point.

WHAT TO DO: Design a rug with a focal point.

1. Select the ☐ or ⬭ shape tool. Draw a large rectangle or circle as the shape of the rug.

2. Select from a variety of tools: Design a rug. Use repeated lines and geometric shapes.

3. Make one part of the rug the center of interest, or focal point, by using location or contrast in line, shape, or color.

Technology Objective: The student uses software programs with graphics to enhance learning experiences.

TECHNOLOGY

Name _____ *Date* _____

INVENTING A STORY FROM DETAILS

Although Leslie has gone from the scene in Fish's painting, she has left many things behind. They clutter the table where she was sitting. What clues do they give you about Leslie?

Be a detective, and try to imagine what Leslie was doing right before she left. Why did she leave? Where did she go? A writer of stories includes a beginning, a middle, and an ending, which introduce a problem, complicate it, and then solve it.

WHAT TO DO: Write a short-short story about the mystery of Leslie. Deduce what she was doing, why she left in haste, and where she went. Build suspense to add interest to your story. Use another sheet of paper if you need more room.

_____

_____

_____

_____

_____

_____

_____

_____

_____

_____

_____

_____

Reading/Language Arts Objectives: The student produces engaging writing (for example, by using dialogue, suspense, etc.). The student writes to develop and record ideas.

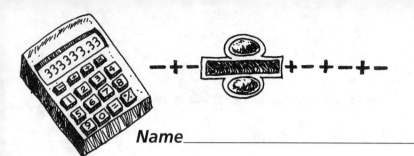

Name_____ Date_____

POSSIBLE COMBINATIONS

An artist may combine numerous different lines, shapes, or colors to create variety in an artwork. For example, imagine your class is making and selling papier-mâché animal mobiles. Each mobile has six animals—three on each arm. You may use these animal shapes in a number of different combinations:

crab   frog   octopus   dolphin   starfish

WHAT TO DO: Answer the questions about possible combinations of animals in the mobiles. Make diagrams to help solve the problems.

1. How many combinations are possible if you use only crabs and

frogs?_____
Show the combinations in a chart like this. Construct your chart on the back of this sheet.

	Number of crabs	Number of frogs
Comb. 1		
Comb. 2		

2. How many combinations are possible if you use dolphins, starfish,

and octopuses? _____
Make a second chart to show these combinations.

3. How many combinations are possible if you use all five animals?

Explain how you know this. _____

_____

_____

_____

_____

Mathematics Objective: The student develops an appropriate problem-solving strategy, including make a table, etc.

Name_____ **Date**_____

A RECYCLING PROJECT

In *She Ba*, Romare Bearden has combined various materials once used for another purpose to create a new artwork. In essence, he has reused materials that we would normally throw away. To *reuse* is to use again. To *recycle* is to make new products out of used materials. Reusing and recycling are valuable because they cut down on waste of resources and conserve, or save, our planet's energy.

WHAT TO DO: Make a collage that expresses your point of view about reusing and recycling. Follow these steps.

1. Think and make notes about ways to conserve resources. On another sheet, make sketches of things that make you think of reusing or recycling materials.

2. Make a list of throwaway materials that you can use in your collage. Select a variety of textures, colors, and shapes.

3. Play with different ways of combining your materials. Consult your notes and sketches. Plan a design or picture that will clearly show your ideas about reusing and recycling.

4. Gather the materials you will need to assemble your collage, such as cardboard or paper, glue, string, scissors, markers, a ruler, and paints.

5. Create your collage. Write a paragraph expressing your ideas about reusing and recycling. Mention any new ways to recycle that have occurred to you. Attach your paragraph to your collage and share it.

Science Objective: The student designs and implements plans for reducing, reusing, and recycling in his or her community.

SCIENCE

Name _____ Date _____

INFORMATION GATHERING

What can you tell about the life of Leslie from the objects in *After Leslie Left*? A society can be analyzed through the objects it makes, uses, collects, or values. An archaeologist uncovers ancient households, categorizes the items found there, and tries to understand what they show about the culture.

WHAT TO DO: List each object in *After Leslie Left* under an appropriate heading. Then, answer the questions.

eating/drinking	cleaning	reading	storing	other

1. Name three things this person spends time doing.

_____

_____

2. Place an **X** beside each statement that you think is supported by the evidence shown in this artwork.

_____ A clean house is important.

_____ Families are better off with a pet.

_____ Fresh fruit is a good snack.

_____ Live plants make a house pleasant.

_____ A wise shopper saves money on household expenses.

_____ Walk whenever you can instead of driving.

_____ Take a break and relax during your day.

_____ Save and reuse resources.

_____ Plastic is better than metal or glass.

_____ Keep your valuables locked up.

Social Studies Objective: The student analyzes contemporary social studies data.

SOCIAL STUDIES

Name _____   Date _____

CHARACTER AND CONFLICT

Can you create a drama out of the things Janet Fish painted in *After Leslie Left*? As the curtain rises on a play, the audience gets clues from the set and the actors as to what the play is going to be about. The opening scene should reveal who the characters are, what they are like, and what problems they have.

WHAT TO DO: Create an opening scene for a play using the setting of *After Leslie Left*. Use these suggestions to help you invent characters and write dialogue and stage directions.

1. Pretend that the objects in the painting are on a table on a stage. You are a maid or butler who enters and sees them. What do you

say? How do you feel? _____

_____

_____

2. What is the drama or conflict that these objects are causing?

_____

_____

3. What other characters do you want to introduce? What do they have

to do with the problem? _____

_____

_____

4. On another sheet of paper, write your opening scene. Dialogue and stage directions look like this:

Maid: Not again! I can't believe it!
(Irritated, Maid crosses briskly to table and begins to tidy with sharp movements.)

THE ARTS

Arts (Theater) Objective: The student creates characters, environments, and actions that create tension and suspense.

*Name*_____ *Date*_____

Artists vary the elements of line, shape, and color to create variety in artwork to add interest.

WHAT TO DO: Create variety in a design with repeating objects.

1. Select from a variety of tools: Draw a common household object.

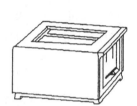

2. Use the ✍ tool to select your object. Choose the Copy and Paste commands from the Edit menu and create and arrange duplicates.

3. Use the 🖐 tool or the 🖌 tool to create variety in the design. Add different lines, shapes, colors, or textures to each shape.

Technology Objective: The student uses software programs with graphics to enhance learning experiences.

TECHNOLOGY

Name _____ Date_____

ELEMENTS THAT UNIFY A POEM

In an artwork, harmony arises from similar shapes, lines, or colors repeated. In a poem, a feeling of harmony comes from uses of similar sounds, line lengths, and stanza shapes. Notice how rhyme, rhythm, and line create harmony and unify this poem, called "Wanting":

As a rule,
Man is a fool.
When it's hot
He wants it cool.
When it's cool
He wants it hot,
Always wanting
What is not.
                    -Anonymous

WHAT TO DO: Write a poem about *Tree House* or *Detroit Industry* with rhyming words. Give your lines rhythm, and write them so that a reader can identify the rhythm easily.

_____

_____

_____

_____

_____

_____

_____

_____

_____

_____

Reading/Language Arts Objectives: The student recognizes distinctive features of genres (poetry). The student writes to inform.

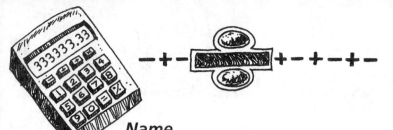

Name_____ Date_____

SIMILAR AND CONGRUENT FIGURES

Related shapes are used in *Tree House* and *Detroit Industry* to unify the artworks. The repeated elements create a feeling of harmony. In mathematics, shapes are *similar* when they have the same shape. They are *congruent* when they have the same size and shape.

WHAT TO DO: For each design, write a **C** inside shapes that are congruent to the one on the left. Write an **S** inside shapes that are similar.

1.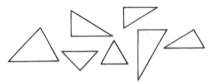

2.

3.

Use the shape pictured below along with one or two others to create a design with harmony. Draw on the back of this sheet of paper. Using color or a pattern of lines, emphasize the congruent shapes.
HINT: Use a ruler and make a template of the shape to keep size and shape exact.

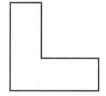

Mathematics Objectives: The student uses critical attributes to define geometric shapes or solids. The student uses translations, reflections, and rotations to make geometric patterns.

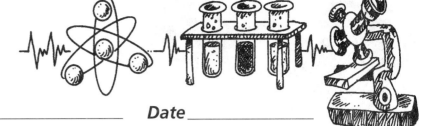

Name _____ Date _____

INTERACTIONS WITHIN AN ECOSYSTEM

The mural *Detroit Industry* shows the mass production of cars in a factory. In *mass production*, each worker or machine on an assembly line does one step in the process of building an object, such as a car or lawn mower. In the mural, teams of workers assemble different parts of the cars. Machines work together harmoniously. Because each worker or machine is able to do one task quickly, mass production *conserves*, or saves, time and energy.

WHAT TO DO: Imagine that you are in charge of a factory that builds bicycles. How will you divide the process of building the bicycles into steps? Describe the task that will be done in each step and the number of workers needed to do each step.

_____

_____

_____

_____

_____

How does the process you have described save energy?

_____

_____

_____

_____

_____

Science Objective: The student designs ways by which energy can be conserved.

Name _____ Date _____

LIVING IN BALANCE WITH NATURE

The painting *Tree House* suggests how the human world and the natural world are interwoven. Elements of nature surround the people shown in the painting.

WHAT TO DO: Complete each activity.

1. Describe the elements of nature—for example, plants and animals—that you see in *Tree House*. _____

_____

_____

_____

2. Describe the relationship between people and the natural environment as shown in the painting. _____

_____

_____

_____

3. Now, read the paragraph below. List at least three ideas that we must take into consideration to solve the problem described.

Large increases in the human population have led to many problems for the environment. Crowding, loss of wildlife habitats, and pollution threaten to upset the balance of nature. Many species could become extinct. Raising adequate food may become a problem. Pollution poisons air, land, and water. What will it take for humans to live in balance with nature? _____

_____

_____

_____

_____

Social Studies Objective: The student applies problem-solving and decision-making skills to the interpretation and resolution of contemporary problems.

202

SOCIAL STUDIES

Name _____ **Date** _____

CHORDS AND HARMONY

In music, harmony results from *chords*—combinations of notes played simultaneously to make a pleasing sound. A chord combines notes from a scale. In most Western music (music of Europe and the Americas), a scale is made up of eight tones named with the letters **A** to **G.**

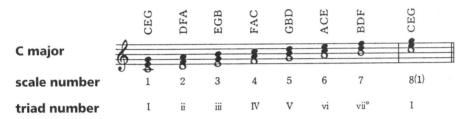

	CEG	DFA	EGB	FAC	GBD	ACE	BDF	CEG
C major								
scale number	1	2	3	4	5	6	7	8(1)
triad number	I	ii	iii	IV	V	vi	vii°	I

In this scale, an *interval* is the distance between two pitches. From **C** to **F** is an interval of a fourth because four letter names lie between them. The simplest type of chord is a *triad*, which combines three notes in intervals of a third. The lowest note is called the *root*, the second tone is called the *third*, and the highest tone is the *fifth*.

WHAT TO DO: Decide which of the following combinations form triads. Put an **X** by each triad. Then, write the musical notation for each triad.

1. BCD

2. BDF

3. GBD

4. FEF

Arts (Music) Objective: The student demonstrates knowledge of the basic principles of chords.

Name_____ Date_____

Artists use the principle of harmony to create unity, the sense or feeling that objects belong together. Harmony is created by using similar elements: lines, shapes, or colors.

WHAT TO DO: Create a scene that shows harmony with color.

1. Select from a variety of tools: 🖌️ ✏️ ☐ ◯ ＼
Draw a variety of favorite objects.

2. Draw a background and use the ✍ tool to select and arrange the shapes in it.

3. Create harmony in the scene with color. Use the 🖐 tool to add different values of one color to the entire scene.

Technology Objective: The student uses software programs with graphics to enhance learning experiences.

204

TECHNOLOGY

LANGUAGE ARTS

*Name*_____ *Date*_____

SUBJECT-VERB AGREEMENT

A work of art shows unity when its parts join in an agreeable way.
The English language calls for agreement between subjects and verbs.
Singular subjects need singular verb forms. Plural subjects take plural
verb forms. *Singular* refers to one; *plural* refers to more than one.

As a rule:
Plural nouns end in *-s*.	My *friends* like pizza.
Singular verbs end in *-s*.	My friend *likes* pizza.
She, he, it are singular.	*He* paints still lifes.
They is plural.	*They* paint still lifes.

WHAT TO DO: Underline the verb in parentheses that agrees with the
subject of each sentence.

1. Artists (try, tries) to give their work a feeling of wholeness, or unity.
2. Similar shapes (give, gives) a feeling of belonging to objects in a
painting.
3. Repetition (become, becomes) a way of creating harmony in art.
4. However, almost any given artwork (contain, contains) great variety.
5. Contrasting elements (bring, brings) interest, but how do they relate
to unity in a work of art?
6. The artist (show, shows) how elements (belong, belongs) together
by showing how they (relate, relates) to one another.

On the back of this page, write a paragraph describing the playground
in the lesson. Underline subjects and verbs you have used. Check to be
sure that they agree.

Reading/Language Arts Objective: The student employs standard English usage in polished formal writing
(for example, attends to subject-verb agreement.)

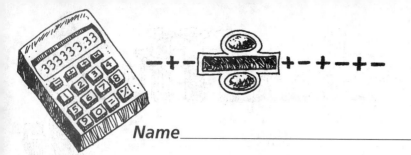

Name_____ Date_____

ESTIMATING DISTANCES

The playground of a park must be well planned for safety and ease of use. Equipment should be located so that there is enough space between pieces. Planners must take into account the type of use and movement generated by each piece of equipment. To get a rough idea about the best placement of playground equipment, designers estimate distances.

WHAT TO DO: Use the map of Timmons Park and the designer's notes to discover the best arrangement of swings and seesaws for the new playground. Estimate the distances to solve the problems below.

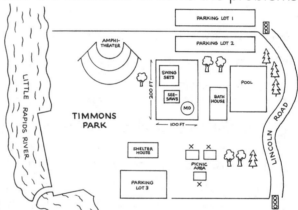

Designer's notes:

6 seesaws - altogether 12 ft. wide and 30 ft. long; leave 10 ft. before and behind seesaws

2 swing sets - each 5 ft. wide and 25 ft. long; side by side, 10 ft. apart; 25 ft. clearance before and behind swings

1 merry-go-round - 8 ft. across; set within circular space 32 ft. across

1. About how much space is required for the swing sets?

_____ feet x _____feet = _____square feet

2. About how much space is required for the seesaws?

_____ feet x _____feet = _____square feet

3. About how far is each parking lot from the swing sets?

Lot 1_____ feet   Lot 2 _____feet   Lot 3 _____feet

Mathematics Objective: The student uses estimation to solve problems where exact answers are not required.

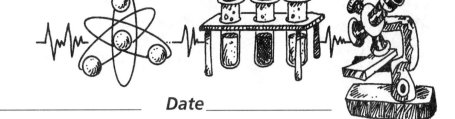

Name_____ Date_____

LEVERS AND FORCE

The seesaw is a familiar item on a playground. It is a kind of lever. A lever is a simple machine made of a bar that *pivots*, or moves about a fixed point when a force is applied. The pivot point is called the *fulcrum*. When an *effort force* is applied, the bar moves about its fulcrum. The effort force must be greater than the *resistance force* at the opposite end of the bar.

WHAT TO DO: Use the picture of the lever and what you know about forces to answer these questions.

1. Explain what happens when one end of a seesaw goes down. Use the words *lever*, *fulcrum*, *effort force*, and *resistance force* in your explanation.

_____

_____

_____

2. What happens to the effort force as arm 1 of the lever gets longer?

_____

_____

3. Which arm should be long for the lighter person on the seesaw?

_____

Science Objective: The student explains the motion of objects as a result of force applied.

SCIENCE

Name _____   *Date* _____

RIGHTS AND RESPONSIBILITIES

The park and playground you have studied in this lesson show unity that comes from the harmony of their parts. These busy public places also maintain harmony by making clear the rights and responsibilities of the people who use them. Rules and laws guide the behavior of park visitors. For example, all people have the right to use the park. They are also responsible for following safety rules and the law. Breaking the rules has consequences: someone breaking a rule or law faces fines or other punishment.

WHAT TO DO: Imagine that you are a member of your community park board. Make a list of the rights of children who use the park. Then, make a list of their responsibilities. Explain the consequences of breaking the rules.

Rights (ways and times children may use the park)

_____

_____

_____

Responsibilities (rules to follow)

_____

_____

_____

Consequences (what happens if a rule is broken)

_____

_____

_____

Social Studies Objectives: The student compares the rights and responsibilities of a citizen of the United States. The student evaluates choices and describes consequences.

SOCIAL STUDIES

Name _____ Date _____

PANTOMIMING HARMONY AND CONFLICT

Pantomime is acting without words. It communicates only through gestures, actions, and expressions. If you were watching children playing from a distance, their play might look like pantomime. Could you tell which children were getting along and which were not?

WHAT TO DO: Think of a playground activity you enjoy with your friends. Describe the body movements, gestures, and facial expressions of the characters. Invent a pantomime that will show this activity in which everyone is playing in unity.

Body movements: _____

_____

Gestures: _____

_____

Expressions: _____

_____

Add a pantomime that shows the same group in conflict.

Body movements: _____

_____

Gestures: _____

_____

Expressions: _____

_____

THE ARTS

Arts (Theater) Objective: The student analyzes and invents character behaviors based on observation of interactions and emotional responses of people.

Name_____ Date_____

Harmony is sameness, but when too much is repeated in an artwork, it becomes uninteresting. Unity is the balance between harmony, or sameness, and variety, or difference.

WHAT TO DO: Create a group theme drawing that balances harmony and variety.

1. As a group, choose a setting for a scene–a desert, underwater, outer space, and so on. Take turns drawing the shape of an object that relates to the theme.

Select from a variety of tools: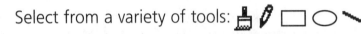

2. Continue taking turns until the scene is complete.

3. Create unity in the scene. Add similar colors or a border.

Use a variety of tools:

Technology Objective: The student uses software programs with graphics to enhance learning experiences.

TECHNOLOGY

Name_____ Date_____

UNIFIED PARAGRAPHS

The unity of the jewelry in this lesson comes from the smooth and functional way the parts fit together. In writing a paragraph, unity comes from the way you make each sentence fit.

- Each detail relates to the immediate topic.
- Sentences are placed in logical order.
- Sentences are joined by transitions, such as *next*, *because*, and *and*.

WHAT TO DO: Read the topic sentence. Put a ✔ beside each detail that supports the topic sentence. Then, number the sentences you checked to show the logical order in which they would appear in a paragraph.

Topic sentence: Scythian tombs in Ukraine reveal the love of an ancient people for beautiful gold objects.

_____ _____ She was adorned in a gold crown, gold bracelets, and gold rings.

_____ _____ A large gold necklace carved with scenes of Scythian life was found in a nobleman's tomb.

_____ _____ In a nearby chamber, searchers discovered the nobleman's wife.

_____ _____ When a king died, Scythians lamented and bloodied themselves as the body was pulled on a wagon.

_____ _____ Although her robe had decayed after 2,600 years, the small rectangular plates of carved gold that had been sewn onto it were still in place.

Reading/Language Arts Objective: The student produces cohesive written forms.

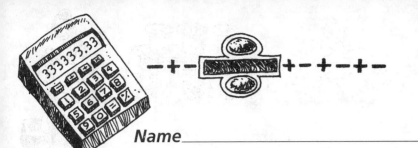

Name_____   Date_____

MEASURING TO MAKE A PATTERN

The jewelry in this lesson was crafted by a careful artist. It took skill in shaping metals and exact measurement to create the pieces.

WHAT TO DO: Pretend you are going to make a necklace like the one below, using string and cardboard. Decide how long each piece of string must be. Measure how large each shape must be.

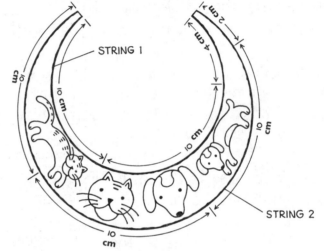

1. Explain how you measured the strings and shapes in the picture.

_____

_____

2. Give the measurements for each strand of string.

_____

_____

3. Measure and write the sizes of each shape in the necklace. Make your measurements in centimeters.

cat face _____

dog face _____

cat body _____

dog body _____

Mathematics Objectives: The student selects an appropriate problem solving strategy. The student uses measurement procedures to solve problems involving length, etc.

Name _____   Date _____

THE MINERAL QUARTZ

Jewelry is often made from gold, silver, and gems. Gems are minerals taken from the earth. Minerals can be identified by their distinctive crystal structure, color, luster, (how they reflect light), hardness, and other traits.

WHAT TO DO: Find out about the mineral quartz from the information below. Then answer the questions.

quartz

Mineral	Hardness
Talc	1
Gypsum	2
Calcite	3
Fluorite	4
Apatite	5
Orthoclase	6
Quartz	7
Topaz	8
Corundum	9
Diamond	10

Categories	Descriptions	Examples
metallic	bright, shiny	gold
glassy	like glass	quartz
brilliant	sparkling	diamond

1. Copper has a hardness of 3.5. Which is harder, quartz or copper?

_____

2. Describe the crystal structure of quartz. How many sides do quartz

crystals have? _____

_____

3. There are several types of quartz gems. Which of the gems described below are quartz? Circle them.
   a. amethyst—orchid to purple in color; six-sided crystal structure
   b. opal—vivid flashes of colored light; hardness of 7; six-sided crystals
   c. zircon—four-sided crystal structure; various colors; brilliant luster

Science Objective: The student applies knowledge of the properties of matter.

Name _____ Date _____

OUR LOVE OF NECKLACES

People usually wear jewelry to decorate themselves, but we often wear it for other reasons. Often people wear religious symbols, organizational symbols, good luck charms, and amulets for protection from sickness and bad luck. Prehistoric people wore necklaces made of natural objects that were strung on leather or reeds. By the late 2000s B.C., Egyptians were making jewelry of metal and gemstones.

WHAT TO DO: Design a necklace that would be important to you. Draw a picture of it. Then, describe it and tell why it is important to you.

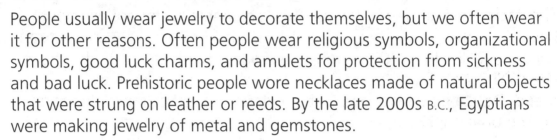

_____

_____

_____

_____

Social Studies Objective: The student recognizes ways various cultures, societies, and individuals meet their needs.

SOCIAL STUDIES

*Name*_____ *Date*_____

THE MYSTERY OF THE MISSING NECKLACE

The necklace is missing! Where is it? Who took it? How will you get it back?

WHAT TO DO: Plan a play about a missing necklace. Work with a friend. Describe the necklace. Then, follow the plan below to create an outline of your play.

Description of the Necklace:_____

_____

Title:_____

Setting:_____

Main Characters:_____

_____

_____

Problem:_____

_____

Plot Summary:_____

_____

_____

_____

Solution to Problem:_____

_____

_____

THE ARTS

Arts (Theater) Objective: The student creates characters, environments, and actions that create tension and suspense.

Name_____ Date_____

Unity is oneness. It makes a picture look complete and satisfying.

WHAT TO DO: Design a piece of jewelry using harmony and variety to create unity.

1. Design a piece of jewelry. Draw a pendant, a ring, a bracelet, a belt buckle, an earring, or another piece. Decide whether the piece will have a combination of geometric and free-form shapes or only one kind of shape, whether it will have formal or informal balance, and whether you use common objects or those in nature.

Select from a variety of tools: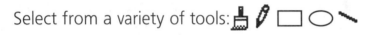

2. Add color and texture.
Select from a variety of tools:

Technology Objective: The student uses software programs with graphics to enhance learning experiences.

TECHNOLOGY

Answer Key

UNIT 1, *Lesson 1*

Reading/Language Arts

curved–from Latin *curvus*...
spiral–from Latin *spira*...
vertical–from Latin *vertic*...
diagonal–from Greek *dia*-...
straight–from Middle English *strecchen*...
horizontal–from Greek *horos*...
Sentences may vary but should contain the following ideas:
1. A spiral is a line that curves around a central point while increasing or decreasing its distance from that point.
2. A diagonal line moves at a slant.
3. A vertical line moves up and down.

Mathematics
1. 15 total diagonal lines; 3 subsets of lines; 5 lines in each subset, division problem:
   $15 \div 3 = 5$
2. 9 total curved lines; 3 subsets of lines; 3 lines in each subset; division problem:
   $9 \div 3 = 3$
3. 6 total zigzag lines; 3 subsets of lines; 2 lines in each subset, division problem:
   $6 \div 3 = 2$

Science
Answers will vary.

Social Studies
Life of weaver: hunt for and raise own food; hut with no light; no running water; travel on foot or by horse; trade for needed items; drought a serious problem; wear hand-woven clothing
Life of factory worker: take paycheck to bank; house with electric lights; running water; wear manufactured clothing; buy food in grocery store; crime a serious problem; car or public transportation

Arts (Dance)
Students practice steps for waltz, then create a pattern of steps for their own dance.

Technology
Students will use drawing and painting programs to draw two pictures using a variety of lines and tools.

UNIT 1, *Lesson 2*

Reading/Language Arts
Answers will vary. Possible answers include the following:
1. The lines are all different lengths.
2. The snowflakes are "dancing rapidly."
3. The poem is describing snow falling at night.

Mathematics
Students mark two triangles with a star; two circles with shading; and two squares with an **X**.

Science
1. They will migrate to the south to find food.
2. They will fly north.
3. Canada and the United States
4. insects and earthworms
5. Because many insects die and the ground is frozen.

Answer Key

Social Studies

1. Bar graph comparing river lengths should show the following information:
   River length in miles
   Nile (Africa) 4,000
   Amazon (South America) 3,900
   Yangtze (China) 3,100
   Mississippi (U.S.A.) 2,500
2. Circle graph showing revenue sources should show the following information:
   Source of income Percent
   Sales and utility taxes 25%
   Property tax 50%
   State income tax 20%
   Other (fines, fees, special services, etc.) 5%

Arts (Music)

1.–4. Answers will vary. Students make up the words and melody for a song.

Technology

Students will use drawing and painting programs to draw a picture using geometric and free-form shapes.

UNIT 1, *Lesson 3*

Reading/Language Arts

Paragraphs will vary. Students identify the apparent contradiction in a paradox and tell why a paradox may yet seem true.

Mathematics

1. a. $\frac{2}{16}$, or $\frac{1}{8}$
   b. $\frac{2}{6}$, or $\frac{1}{3}$
   c. $\frac{8}{6}$, or $\frac{4}{3}$
   d. $\frac{6}{10}$, or $\frac{3}{5}$
2. Circle: $\frac{1}{1}$
   Kite: $\frac{1}{2}$

Science

Chart:
Fish; gills take in oxygen from water, feed on plants and other animals; get water from lakes, rivers, wells they live in
People; breathe air with lungs; eat plants and animals; sometimes hunt for food, sometimes trade for food; get water from body of water
Answers will vary. Students invent an imaginary animal, describe its survival needs and how they are met, and draw the animal.

Social Studies

Answers will vary. Possible answers:
1. They were formed to help elect government leaders.
2. The parties provide platforms consisting of ideas and solutions to problems.
3. They help in selecting lawmakers at the local level.

Arts (Theater)

Answers will vary. Students create a stage set for a play based on the painting Deidre. They should make notes regarding the scenery, lighting, costumes, and props for the play.

Technology

Students will use drawing and painting programs to create value scales and a three-dimensional object from different viewpoints.

UNIT 1, *Lesson 4*

Reading/Language Arts

Journal entries will vary. Students write from the point of view of someone in a painting by Elizabeth Catlett or Käthe Kollwitz.

Answer Key

Mathematics
a. (1,4)
b. (3,5)
c. (6,6)
d. (8,4)
e. (8,2)
f. (6,1)
g. (2,2)

Science
1. Describe how each level of darkness in the scale was created.
2. Step A 4 /   0 \   Step D 8 /   8 \
   Step B 4 /   4 \   Step E 16 /   8 \
   Step C 8 /   4 \   Step F 16 /   16 \
3. Increase the number of slanted lines, first in one direction and then in both directions.
4. Students test the method they described in item 3.
5. Answers may vary.

Social Studies
first caption: Plantations use African-Americans as laborers.
second caption: Landowners rent to sharecroppers.
third caption: Farmers use machinery to plant and harvest.
Reports will vary. Students research and report on farming methods in the South today and 100 years ago.

Arts (Music)
1. Answers will vary. Possible answers: hope or sadness. Explanations will vary.
2. Explanations may vary.
3. repetition; strong rhythm; accented by gestures; clear, strong emotion; solo and chorus refrain

Technology
Students will use drawing and painting programs to draw a picture with light and dark values.

UNIT 1, *Lesson 5*

Reading/Language Arts
Order may vary. Suggested order:
2, 6, 3, 4, 1, 9, 5, 7, 8
Paragraphs will vary. Check for transition words.

Mathematics
Students circle one rectangular solid, two cubes, one pyramid. Volumes are as follows:
Rectangular solid: 3 x 2 x 4 = 24
First cube: 3 x 3 x 3 = 9
Second rectangular solid: 2 x 5 x 4 = 40
Second cube: 4 x 4 x 4 = 64
Answers will vary. Students find a three-dimensional object and measure it and calculate its volume.

Science
1. All the light rays are reflected at an angle that is equal and opposite to the angle at which they struck the surface.
2. The light rays are all reflected in different directions.
3. the diagram of light reflected off a smooth surface.
4. the diagram of light reflected off a rough surface.
5. Designs may vary but should show mirrors parallel to each other inside each end of a cardboard tube. The mirrors should be arranged at an angle inside the tube so that light entering one end of the tube will be reflected to the mirror at the other end.

Social Studies
1. a. Spain
   b. Mexico
   c. United States
2. the Red River and the Rio Grande
3. Louisiana, Arkansas, Oklahoma, New Mexico

Answer Key

Arts (Music)

1. Answers will vary. Students might mention that people today still enjoy live musical performances, but that people like the girls in the painting would not have listened to music on the radio or on television.
2.–4. Answers will vary.

Technology

Students will use drawing and painting programs to create highlights and shadows in a picture of a classmate.

UNIT 1, *Lesson 6*

Reading/Language Arts

Paragraphs will vary but should demonstrate the use of different sentence lengths and structures to contrast ideas.

Mathematics

Patterns will vary. Students first draw a pattern using lines and geometric shapes; then they copy the pattern by measuring the shapes in the original and reproducing them.

Science

1. book; 2; Students circle 1 kg.
2. cat food; 4; Students circle 2 kg.
3. tractor; 10; Students circle 1500 kg.

Social Studies

1900: less than 500,000 cars in America; 20-mph speeds; hand brakes; two-cylinder engines; natural rubber tires; hand crank to start

1950: more have cars than do not; eight-cylinder engines; synthetic rubber tires; automatic ignition; high-beam headlights; 60-mph speeds; disk brakes

NOW: 120-mph speeds; seat belts and air bags; buy new car frequently; antilock braking system; computerized controls; radial tires

Paragraphs will vary.

Arts (Theater)

1.–4. Answers will vary. Students create a character appropriate for a setting such as that shown in American Rural Baroque.

Technology

Students will use drawing and painting programs to create shapes by using shading techniques.

Answer Key

UNIT 2, *Lesson 1*

Reading/Language Arts
1. Answers will vary. Possible answers: place and date of birth, size and circumstances of family, educational experience, achievements, and people who influenced King's early development.
2. Answers will vary. Possible answers: higher education, marriage and family, jobs, and rise to leadership role.
3. Answers will vary. Possible answers: encyclopedias, biographies, television documentaries, news articles, and so on.
4. Answers will vary. Possible answers: other civil rights leaders or family members or friends who remember the period of King's life.
5. Answers will vary. Possible answers: anecdotes and facts about King's actions and speeches, tributes written by others, and King's reputation today.

Mathematics
1. 384 miles
2. 1,730 miles
3. 822 miles
4. 3,407 miles

Science
Answers will vary. Students describe materials, tools, and steps needed to make a map without using paper or pencils. They may describe maps made with wax or other materials that could be molded.

Social Studies
1. Questions will vary.
2. Posters, poems, and reports about King will vary.

Arts (Music)
1. Answers will vary. Possible answers: pride, hope, and patriotic feelings.
2. Verses will vary.
3. Students sing the new verse they wrote.

Technology
Students will use drawing and painting programs to create monochromatic motifs.

UNIT 2, *Lesson 2*

Reading/Language Arts
Descriptions will vary but could include the following:
A large, smooth pink stone with an egg shape sits in the center of the top two-thirds of the picture. Jawbone and teeth are in the foreground. Answers will vary.

Mathematics
1. 397.06
2. 1,104.49
3. The total for yellow and its analogous colors is greater.

Science
Loom designs may vary but could use cardboard as frame, with warp threads anchored around it. Students weave together yarn or strips of colored paper.

Answer Key

Social Studies
1. 75°-90°.
2. dry, hot, desert, rural, mountainous, range land, mesa
3. from 0 to 25
4. raising livestock
5. Answers will vary. Possible answers: the following: In the mountains and during colder parts of the year, people needed blankets and clothing to keep them warm. They learned to use the wool from their herds of sheep to make these items.

Arts (Music)
Answers may vary.

Technology
Students will use drawing and painting programs to create designs using analogous colors.

UNIT 2, *Lesson 3*

Reading/Language Arts
Opinions and supporting facts may vary but could include the following:
Opinion: I do not think it is a good idea to serve fast food for lunch at school.
Supporting fact: Fast food tends to be high in fat.
Supporting fact: Fast food tends to include fewer fresh fruits and vegetables.
Supporting fact: Fast food is often high in calories.
Opposite side: I think it is a good idea to serve fast food for lunch at school.
Supporting fact: Fast-food service will save the schools money.

Mathematics
1. hexagon: 2 triangles, 1 rectangle or 4 triangles
   parallelogram: 2 triangles or 1 square and 2 triangles
   trapezoid: 1 rectangle and 1 triangle, or 2 triangles, or 3 triangles
2. triangle; square; rectangle; hexagon
3. Polygons and descriptions will vary.

Science
1. The feathers were difficult to obtain– someone probably had to walk or ride several hundred miles to a forest to get them.
2. The neckpiece probably belonged to an important person. That it was made of rare materials and that it was found in a burial ground suggest this.
3. The use of cotton backing indicates that cotton was cultivated.

Social Studies
1. silk, linen, wool, and cotton
2. rayon, nylon, and polyester
3. wool and linen
4. wool and silk

Arts (Dance)
Answers will vary. Students develop a ritual dance for an important occasion and devise a costume and other adornments to be worn for the dance.

Technology
Students will use drawing and painting programs to draw a mask using complementary colors.

Answer Key

UNIT 2, *Lesson 4*

Reading/Language Arts
1. sad; depressed
2. large city, especially one that is a large commercial or cultural center
3. a large, sad-looking city
4. mel' an chol' y; me trop' o lis
5. suggestive of heat or warmth, as in the *warm* colors red and orange
6. Answers will vary. Possible answers: meaning, pronunciation, part of speech, and syllabication.

Mathematics
1. 420 creatures
2. 8 baskets
3. $60.00
4. 40 feet

Science
1. Alkaid, Mizar, Alioth, Megrez, Phecda, Merak, and Dubhe
2. Answers may vary. Probable answers:
   Dubhe: 5, 5.5; 4.5, 7.5
   Merak: 6, 5.5; 5.5, 7.5
   Phecda: 5.5, 4; 5.5, 6.5
   Alioth: 4.5, 3.5; 5, 5.5
3. No.
4. The location of the constellation in the sky changes over time; the positions of the stars in relation to one another remain the same.

Social Studies
Plans for and descriptions of mural will vary.

Arts (Theater)
Answers will vary.

Technology
Students will use drawing and painting programs to draw technical design using warm and cool colors.

UNIT 2, *Lesson 5*

Reading/Language Arts
1. a.
2. Hieroglyphs can be read left to right.
3. Answers will vary.

Mathematics
1. Both calendars have twelve months.
2. Our calendar has months of 28, 30, and 31 days. The Egyptian calendar has only 30-day months.
3. 52 weeks, 7 days, 365 or 366 days

Science
1. physical
2. chemical
3. physical
4. Answers will vary.

Social Studies
1. Most Egyptians lived along the Nile because they would have a water source and the land was fertile.
2. It made farming possible in a desert land.
3. Answers will vary.

Arts (Dance)
Answers will vary but may include:
1. a. wild, boogying, free, fast
   b. stiff, graceful, unbending, slow, angular
2.–4. Dances and music will vary.

Technology
Students will use drawing and painting programs to draw designs that show rhythm.

Answer Key

UNIT 2, *Lesson 6*

Reading/Language Arts
Answers will vary.

Mathematics
1. exact
2. estimate
3. estimate
4. estimate
5. estimate
6. exact
7. Estimates and actual measurements will vary.

Science
Answers will vary but might include:
Characteristics of water shoes: waterproof, lightweight, durable
Materials for making shoes: rubber, plastic, nylon

Social Studies
1. The plow cleared the land for farming.
2. Sod houses were used because trees were few and far between.
3. Pioneers left Kansas because the hot, dry weather prevented them from farming.
4. the grasshopper plague

Arts (Theater)
Answers and dialogues will vary.

Technology
Students will use drawing and painting programs to draw a picture using visual rhythm to express mood.

UNIT 3, *Lesson 1*

Reading/Language Arts
1. limestone, crayon, acid
2. Printers use computers and electronic copiers.
3. Answers will vary but may state that lithography is a form of art.

Mathematics
1. Students shade the space within the larger circle on the first figure and the inside circle on the second figure.
2. Students shade the hexagon because it has the larger space within the frame.
3. Estimates will vary. The area is 450 square meters (30 x 15 = 450). It will not cover the 500 square meter field.

Science
1. The lion might not be able to distinguish a zebra clearly enough to pounce on it.
2. Students draw a pattern of spots on the giraffe.
3. Students draw a small pattern on the fish and color it in shades of pink, tan, and black.

Social Studies
1. Pyrenees Mountains
2. Portugal
3. Africa
4. Students draw arrows to Malaga on the southern coast and Barcelona on the eastern coast.
5. Bay of Biscay, Mediterranean Sea, Atlantic Ocean
6. Answers will vary but include Florida, Italy, and Arabia.

Arts (Theater)
One-person plays will vary.

Answer Key

Technology
Students will use drawing and painting programs and use positive and negative space to create a shape reversal.

UNIT 3, *Lesson 2*

Reading/Language Arts
1.–5. Answers will vary.

Mathematics
1. Each fraction is 1/2 of the previous one. The next two fractions in the pattern are 1/32 and 1/64.
2. Each decimal is 0.3 more than the previous one. The next two decimals in the pattern are 1.3 and 1.6.
3. Nicaragua, Canada, Mexico, Japan, United States

Science
Answers will vary but may include:
1. I need to know what prevents the baby turtles from reaching the water.
2. I need to know why the poachers can't get food any other way. I need to know why the poachers don't realize that the sea turtles are endangered.
3. I need to know if the poachers can make money another way. I need to know why the poachers are allowed to steal the turtle eggs.
4. I need to know why there are fewer beaches where sea turtles can lay their eggs. I need to know how to make the beaches safe for the sea turtles.
5. I need to know why fishers don't use a different kind of net. I need to know why fishers don't release the turtles caught by mistake.

Social Studies
Answers will vary.

Arts (Dance)
1. Answers will vary. Possible answers: slink, crawl, wiggle, scurry.
2.–6. Answers will vary.

Technology
Students will use drawing and painting programs to create a tessellation design.

UNIT 3, *Lesson 3*

Reading/Language Arts
Dialogues will vary.

Mathematics
Patterns will vary but should include reflections and rotations of basic geometric patterns.

Science
1.–5. Answers will vary.

Social Studies
1. Students draw a time line from 5,000 B.C. to A.D. 2000 to show the history of textiles.
2. Answers will vary.

Arts (Music)
1.–5. Answers and ballads will vary.

Technology
Students will use drawing and painting programs to draw a room inside a house with visual texture.

Answer Key

UNIT 3, *Lesson 4*

Reading/Language Arts
1.–5. Answers will vary

Mathematics
1. Voyager 1 took 5 months longer to arrive near Jupiter.
2. Voyager 1 came 230,000 miles nearer to Jupiter than Voyager 2.
3. Voyager 2 came 15,000 miles nearer to Saturn than Voyager 1.
4. 144 months

Science
1. Answers will vary. Possible answers: lift weights, do push-ups, do chin-ups.
2. Answers will vary. Possible answers: climb in and out of cars delivering packages, wash windows, cut the grass, sweep the floor.
3. Answers will vary but should support the idea that people in the past did physical work and therefore did not choose to exercise for recreation.
4. Answers will vary.

Social Studies
1. western
2. eastern
3. South Platte River
4. Answers will vary but should include the concept that shading shows different land forms.

Arts (Music)
Musical compositions will vary.

Technology
Students will use drawing and painting programs to draw a space home or space station using a variety of textures.

UNIT 3, *Lesson 5*

Reading/Language Arts
Story and drawings will vary but should be written at a first-grade level.

Mathematics
1. The north and west sides have the best view. Answers will vary. Possible answers: living/family room, kitchen, bedrooms.
2. The north and west sides will be the quietest.
   Answers will vary. Possible answers: bed rooms, study.
3. Answers will vary but house cannot be larger than 400 square feet (the size of the lot).
4. Answers will vary but must take into consideration the size of the lot (400 square feet).
5. Answers will vary. Possible answers: wood, stucco, brick.
6. Answers and sketches will vary.

Science
Questions will vary but might include: Where will the homes be built? Will farm land be used to build homes? Are the rivers big enough to provide water for additional homes? Is the pool big enough for 40 more families to use? Is there room in the town for additional houses? Do the residents of Water Station want more people in their town? What is the school situation in Water Town? Is there adequate electricity to support more buildings?

Social Studies
Answers will vary.

Arts (Dance)
Barn-raising dances will vary but students should demonstrate unified movements.

Answer Key

Technology

Students will use drawing and painting programs to draw a building using architectural forms.

UNIT 3, *Lesson 6*

Reading/Language Arts

1. Plans will vary.
2.–6. Ideas will vary but each group should have supporting reasons for their plan.

Mathematics

1. 17,540,000
2. The range of population is 5,342,000. The median population is 2,350,000.
3. The range of area is 2,432,000 sq. km. The median area is 892,500 sq. km.
4. Population per square kilometer of each state:
   New South Wales—about seven people; Queensland—about two people; South Australia—about one person; Victoria—about nineteen people; Tasmania—about seven people; Western Australia—less than one person

Science

Time lines may vary.
Explanations and predictions will vary but students should offer supporting reasons.

Social Studies

Answers will vary.

Arts (Theater)

Answers will vary but might include:

1. Mercy pants and wipes her hand across forehead. She runs and gasps as the cold water hits her. She shivers and shakes from the cool refreshing water. She sticks out her tongue to get a drink.
2. Kwok walks cautiously with one hand moving gingerly across the top of the fence. He pulls his hand away quickly when he touches the jagged edge of the fence.
3. Ben tiptoes and hops along the beach. He winces every once in a while from the heat of the hot sand.
4. Marcella puts on her new dress and twirls around. As she admires herself in the mirror, she scratches her neck and then twists around to see what is causing the itch. She looks over each shoulder and fumbles along the neckline of her dress until she feels the tag.

Technology

Students will use drawing and painting programs to design a public building.

Answer Key

UNIT 4, *Lesson 1*

Reading/Language Arts

1. Jack was happy to trade the cow for some magic beans; he did not see that the cow was worth more than the beans and that he and his mother needed money more than magic beans. His mother was not pleased because she wanted money for the cow.
2. The mouse thought freedom was important. The story/fable showed that little friends make great friends.
3. Answers will vary. Example might be of a child crying for another toy in the toy store when he or she has a room full of toys at home.
4. The grasshopper thought fun and excitement were important. The ant thought survival and/or planning was important.

Mathematics

1. 2:4
2. 1/2
3. a. 225 centimeters tall
   b. 45 cm
   c. 1/7; Kim is probably closer to her adult size, so the proportion of her head to her height will be close to that of an adult.

Science

Answers will vary according to investigation.
1. Red, orange, yellow, green, blue, purple
2. Red pigment reflects light waves in the red–or longer–range of wavelengths.
3. The blue filter will subtract from other wavelengths, giving all other wavelengths a bluish cast.

Social Studies

Students list selected events on time line in chronological order.

1. The changes in both countries led to new forms of government.
2. Americans were fighting against the English throne; the war in France was a civil war.

Arts (Theater)

Charts and monologues will vary.

Technology

Students will use drawing and painting programs to create a proportional drawing of a teacher or classmate.

UNIT 4, *Lesson 2*

Reading/Language Arts

Short stories will vary.

Mathematics

1. rectangle, triangle, pyramid, cylinder
2. Pictures will vary but should include 3 regular polyhedrons, spheres, and parts of spheres.

Science

Answers will vary but make-believe animal should have qualities that would allow it to live in the selected ecosystem.

Social Studies

Students create bar graphs to show the relative heights of the mountains.

Arts (Theater)

Answers will vary.

Technology

Students will use drawing and painting programs to draw a scene that shows an unrealistic scale.

Answer Key

UNIT 4, *Lesson 3*

Reading/Language Arts
Letters will vary but should follow the form for a business letter.

Mathematics
1. art: lines of symmetry drawn through square, isosceles triangle, star
2. art: lines of symmetry drawn through beetle and bird
3. An artist would not draw a symmetrical face in a realistic portrait because the human body is not perfectly symmetrical.
4. no

Science
1. nose
2. eye
3. tongue
4. skin
5. ear
6. Answers will vary.
7. Answers will vary.
8. Answers will vary.
9. Piece of fruit; blade of grass. Different senses tell you different information–for example, whether flower is real.

Social Studies
Answers will vary.

Arts (Music)
Answers will vary.

Technology
Students will use drawing and painting programs to draw a front and side view of a head in proportion.

UNIT 4, *Lesson 4*

Reading/Language Arts
1.–2. Sentences will vary.

Mathematics
1. Admission and Tickets to special exhibit purchased separately–$56.50
   Regular Family Membership and Tickets to special exhibit–$80.50
   Special Family Membership–$70.00
2. Student choices and explanations will vary.

Science
1. marble; because it is hard and long lasting
2. Chalk, clay, and graphite are media an artist would use.
3. Answers will vary. Possible answers: chalk, clay, graphite, talc.
4. Answers will vary.

Social Studies

Arts (Dance)
Dances will vary.

Technology
Students will use drawing and painting programs to create a cartoon character using exaggeration to show a mood or expression.

UNIT 4, *Lesson 5*

Reading/Language Arts
Speeches will vary but students should avoid all forms of distortion.

Answer Key

Mathematics

1. The ends of the line meet.
2. The möbius strip has two sides.
3. Right-handed overhand knot–3 points; left-handed overhand knot–2 points
4. Answers will vary but should include the concept that a torus is a circle that revolves around an axis that does not intersect it.

Science

1. Answers will vary. Possible answers: The animals would be frightened, scared, or unaware of the predator.
2. Moas were easy to hunt because they could not fly.
3. Deer could eat plants of an environment and destroy the food source for native animals.

Social Studies

Answers will vary.

Arts (Music)

Distortions of voice and instruments sounds will vary.

Technology

Students will use drawing and painting programs to create an expressive mask with distorted features.

UNIT 4, *Lesson 6*

Reading/Language Arts

Stories will vary.

Mathematics

Answers will vary.

Science

1. Answers will vary but might include seat belts or air bags.
2. Seat belts can prevent injuries to passengers.
3. Answers will vary. Possible answers: dousing matches in water.
4. Answers will vary.

Social Studies

1. The pose of the statue and his weapons and armor make Balboa look heroic.
2.–4. Answers and drawings will vary.

Arts (Theater)

Answers and pantomimes will vary.

Technology

Students will use drawing and painting programs to draw a person in a familiar setting using realistic proportions.

UNIT 5, *Lesson 1*

Reading/Language Arts

1. Divide the sentence between country and but.
2. Divide the sentence between you and rather.
3. Write: all bark and no bite.
4. Write: I had no shoes, a man who had no feet. Divide the sentence between shoes and until.
5. Write: comes in like a lion, go out like a lamb.
   Divide the sentence between lion and it.
6. Write: all work, no play.
7. Sentences will vary.

Mathematics

Rotate and flip figures to find congruency.

Answer Key

Science

1. pistil
2. Pollen
3. insects
4. petals, nectar
5. pistil
6. fruit

Social Studies

1. Answers may vary but should mention armlike structure and abilities: reaching, grasping, lifting, circling, tightening.
2. a. taken away routine jobs
   b. required re-education and training
   c. made more products available, created need for skilled workers
3. Answers will vary.

Arts (Dance)

Answers will vary.

Technology

Students will use drawing and painting programs to draw a symmetrically balanced creature scene.

UNIT 5, *Lesson 2*

Reading/Language Arts

1. dumbe–dumb, downe–down, shew–show, leaues–leaves, queene–queen, poyson–poison, viall–vial, powres–pours, commeth–comes
2. He uses them for any noun he wishes to emphasize. We capitalize proper nouns and the first word in a sentence.

Mathematics

Answers will vary, but should be equal.

Science

1. Artist 1 will swing to the right until gravity pushes the figure down. Force will carry artist 1 back toward the platform.
2. Artist 2 will hold 1's feet and both will swing back toward the first platform. Gravity and the forward push of 2 are working.
3. Artists 1 and 2 will swing left until gravity pushes them down. Their forward push will carry them to the right.

Social Studies

Explanations will vary.

Arts (Theater)

Answers will vary.

Technology

Students will use drawing and painting programs to create a still life with informal balance.

UNIT 5, *Lesson 3*

Reading/Language Arts

Some rewordings may vary.

What gives an object value as art? Does it have to be hanging on the wall of a museum? Does it have to be expensive? Some believe there is artistic value in common, ordinary objects around us. For example, look around your kitchen at a pitcher, a vase, and a bowl. Although they may be plain and humble, we can look at them as works of art. In fact, their honest, straightforward plainness makes them beautiful. If their form is true to the function they perform, they have value. This value will stand the test of time.

Answer Key

Mathematics
1. 1 double arc + 3 teardrops + 1 double arc + 3 teardrops
2. 1 square + 2 circles + 3 squares + 4 circles + 5 squares + 6 circles

Science

	Number of Petals	Number of Stamens
stonecrop	5	10
trillium	3	6
garden pea	5	10
lily	6	6
crocus	3	3

Students mark an **X** beside statement 3.

Social Studies
1. for eating/silversmith
2. for warmth/colonial housewife
3. for cooking, laundry, soap making/blacksmith
4. for cider, ale, flour/cooper
5. for entertainment/colonial woman

Arts (Music)
Explanations will vary. Students may mention repeated phrases within each stanza linking its parts. Each stanza shares the same general pattern (cherry, chicken, ring, baby). Each is linked to the next by form and content.

Technology
Students will use drawing and painting programs to create a design with radial balance.

UNIT 5, *Lesson 4*

Reading/Language Arts
1. close-up
2. distant
3. close-up
4. distant
   Descriptions will vary.

Mathematics
1. 7:45 A.M.
2. 6:15 P.M.
3. 12:00 Noon
4. Yes, but he should make back-up arrangements.

Science
1. true
2. false
3. true
4. true
5. false
6. true
7. true

Social Studies
1. b
2. a
3. c
4. a
5.–8. Answers will vary.

Arts (Theater)
Answers will vary.

Technology
Students will use drawing and painting programs to create a peaceful landscape using perspective techniques.

Answer Key

UNIT 5, *Lesson 5*

Reading/Language Arts
Answers will vary but should emphasize manual labor and constant work.

Mathematics
1. Placement of some crops may vary.
2. corn–2/8 or 1/4
   tomatoes–2/8 or 1/4
   peas–1/8
   lettuce and radishes–1/8
   pumpkins and squash–2/8 or 1/4
3. corn and tomatoes
4. 2/8 or 1/4
5. yes
6. 120

Science
Answers will vary, but students should focus on
Land Changes: erosion changes, different vegetation
Changes in the Use of the land: different crops, trees (orchard)
Changes in Buildings: silos, machine sheds, automated dairy barn
Changes in Machinery and Technology: tractors, harvesting machinery, automatic feeders, warmers, furnaces
Changes in Population and Neighbors: more people, houses, and businesses
Drawings will vary.

Social Studies
St. Peter's: grand, intricate, arched, rich, stone, sculpted, ornate, enormous, built for religious reasons, luxurious, expensive
Cornell Farm: practical, angular, plain, simple, wooden, just big enough, made for people or animals, beautiful
Answers will vary.

Arts (Music)
1. Follow the Big Dipper that points to the North Star and eventual freedom.
2. Answers will vary. Possible answers: by going north, following the North Star, a slave could become a free person.
3.–4. Answers will vary.

Technology
Students will use drawing and painting programs to draw a scene using linear perspective techniques.

UNIT 5, *Lesson 6*

Reading/Language Arts
Answers will vary.

Mathematics
1. cylinder–front view
2. cone–overhead view
3. prism–side view
4. pyramid–overhead view

Science
Answers will vary.
1. jet engine
2. vacuum cleaner, loud music, jet engine
3. They avoid pain and hearing loss.
4. Answers will vary.

Social Studies
1. Atlantic states, along the Eastern seaboard
2. west
3. between 1880, and 1890
4. Answers may vary but should mention reliable transportation, linking the whole country, allowing supplies and goods to move west, and allowing the settlement of the west.

Answer Key

Arts (Music)

1. Each song has to do with the railroad.
2. The rhythm imitates a train and sets the tempo and beat for the workers hammering the ties in place.
3. Answers will vary.

Technology

Students will use drawing and painting programs to draw an indoor or outdoor scene from two points of view.

UNIT 6, *Lesson 1*

Reading/Language Arts

1. sugary
2. distress
3. cover up
4. wintry blast
5. parching thirst
6. quiet pond
   Sentences will vary.

Mathematics

Circle: 3,7
Star: 5,3
Moon: 7,6

Science

1. a. cirrus
   b. cumulus
   c. stratus
2. stratus, cumulus, cirrus
3. fair weather
4. Rain will come.

Social Studies

Paragraphs will vary.

Arts (Dance)

Answers will vary.

Technology

Students will use drawing and painting programs to create a personal logo with emphasis.

UNIT 6, *Lesson 2*

Reading/Language Arts

Crows are unusually sociable animals. You may never have thought of having a crow as a pet, but they can make good ones. Paragraphs will vary.

Mathematics

1. 25
2. 24 inches
3. 36 inches
4. 75 feet
5. 25 yards

Science

1. Fibers interlock and air spaces in the core of fibers insulate.
2. Cortical cells are elastic because of folded molecular structure.
3. Each fiber has air spaces at its core.

Social Studies

Paragraphs will vary. Students will mention getting new food sources that required more settled life and learning weaving and jewelry-making skills from neighboring friends and enemies.

Answer Key

Arts (Music)
1. Play these notes softly.
2. Play louder.
3. Gradually play louder for four notes. Play fifth note short and sharp.
4. Gradually become softer.
5. Play softly.

Technology
Students will use drawing and painting programs to design a rug with a focal point.

UNIT 6, Lesson 3

Reading/Language Arts
Stories will vary. Accept stories that successfully integrate many details from the artwork.

Mathematics
1. five
   Combination 1: 1, 5
   Combination 2: 2, 4
   Combination 3: 3, 3
   Combination 4: 4, 2
   Combination 5: 5, 1
2. ten
   Chart should reflect ten different combinations.
3. Five. Only one slot will vary, and it can only be changed five times.

Science
Students make a collage.

Social Studies
food/drink: bananas, cup of coffee, pitcher
cleaning: spray cleaner, sponge, feather duster
reading: magazines, coupons
storing: bowl, plastic wrap
other: keys, plant
1. clipping coupons, cleaning house, reading home-related magazines
2. X A clean house is important.
   X Fresh fruit is a good snack.
   X Live plants make the house more pleasant.
   X A wise shopper saves money on household expenses.
   X Take a break and relax during the day.
   X Plastic is better than metal or glass.

Arts (Theater)
Answers will vary.

Technology
Students will use drawing and painting programs to create variety in a design of repeating objects.

UNIT 6, *Lesson 4*

Reading/Language Arts
Poems will vary.

Mathematics
1. 1 **C**   3 **S**
2. 2 **C**   11 **S**
3. 3 **C**   2 **S**
Drawings will vary.

Science
Answers will vary.

Answer Key

Social Studies
Answers will vary.

Arts (Music)
Two and three are triads.

Technology
Students will use drawing and painting programs to create a scene that shows harmonious use of color.

UNIT 6, *Lesson 5*

Reading/Language Arts
1. try
2. give
3. becomes
4. contains
5. bring
6. shows, belong, relate
   Paragraphs will vary.

Mathematics
1. 60 feet x 55 feet = 3,300 square feet
2. 30 feet x 32 feet = 960 square feet
3. Estimates will vary but should be reasonable.

Science
1. One person applies an effort force on one end of the seesaw. The seesaw pivots on the fulcrum (bar) and lifts the other person (the resistance force).
2. As arm 1 gets longer, the effort force is multiplied. (You can lift a greater resistance force.)
3. The arm on which he or she sits should be longer.

Social Studies
Answers will vary.

Arts (Theater)
Answers will vary.

Technology
Students will use drawing and painting programs to create a group theme drawing that balances harmony and variety.

UNIT 6, *Lesson 6*

Reading/Language Arts
✓ 3 She was adorned in a gold diadem, gold bracelets, and gold rings on every finger.
✓ 1 The large gold necklace carved with scenes of Scythian life was found in a noble man's tomb.
✓ 2 In an adjoining chamber searchers discovered the nobleman's wife.
✓ 5 When a king died, Scythians lamented and bloodied themselves as the body was pulled on a wagon.
✓ 4 Although her robe had decayed over 2,600 years, the small rectangular plates of carved gold that had been sewn onto it were still in place.
Students will rewrite the paragraph, adding transitions where necessary.

Mathematics
1. Measure curved lines with a string that was measured with a cm ruler. Use paper strip measured the same way for the width/length of forms.
2. #1–24 cm, #2–32 cm
3. cat face–2 cm x 2 1/2 cm; dog face–2 3/4 cm x 2 3/4 cm; cat body–5 cm x 2 1/3 cm; dog body–5 cm x 2 cm

Answer Key

Science
1. quartz
2. It is hexagonal (6-sided).
3. a. amethyst
   b. opal

Social Studies
Designs will vary.

Arts (Theater)
Answers will vary.

Technology
Students will use drawing and painting programs to design a piece of jewelry.

Teacher Notes

Teacher Notes

Teacher Notes